The Changing of America
1945 to the Present

Joseph M. Siracusa
University of Queensland

The Forum Press, Inc.
Arlington Heights, Illinois 60004

Library of Congress Cataloging in Publication Data

Siracusa, Joseph M.

    Bibliography: p.
    Includes index.
    1. United States—Politics and government—
    1945–   .
2. United States—History—1945–   . I. Title.
E743.S544   1986   973.92   85-22824
ISBN 0-88273-116-5

Cover illustration: United States nuclear test explosion in
the Pacific, July 23, 1956. Official U.S. Navy Photo.

Manufactured in the United States of America

90 89 88 87 86 MG 1 2 3 4 5 6 7 8 9 10

The Changing of America: 1945 to the Present

Vincent P. DeSantis
General Editor

This book is for my children

Contents

Preface

I have sought in the following pages to write a brief, narrative history of America between 1945 and the present, that is, the period between Harry S. Truman and Ronald Reagan. Organizing my chapters around the various administrations, I have attempted to focus on the changing character of American society, the changing responsibilities Americans have undertaken abroad, and the way Americans have seen themselves as reformers at home. Within this framework I have concentrated principally though not exclusively on political reform, social change, civil rights, the women's movement, nuclear arms control, and the Cold War.

Throughout this exercise I have discovered the extent to which American society has pursued the true, the good, and the beautiful, with more or less success. For example, while it is by no means true that blacks and other minorities in America are participating fully in the American Dream, it is fair to say that blacks, minorities, and women, too, have come to participate in American national life in the 1980s in a manner that could hardly have been imagined in the 1940s. And while American society has changed in its view of itself, American foreign policy, its external outlook, has also changed dramatically. In the 1980s, as was the case in the 1940s, the United States is once again seeking a redefinition of its proper relationship with the outside world, a reaction in large measure to the Vietnam War as well as to a growing concern with the nuclear arms race—perhaps the single most important issue of our times.

Like others engaged in a similar enterprise, I am indebted to many people. I should first like to thank Vincent DeSantis of the University of Notre Dame, the general editor of this series, for his constant encouragement and support. I should also like to thank Mrs. Margaret Lee, my research assistant, employed under the auspices of the Australian Research Grants Commission, for her extensive trips to the library on my behalf, and I must apologize in the same breath for asking her to look at more microfilm than I should have chosen for myself. I should like to thank my colleague, Leopold Launitz-Schurer, for reading and improving parts of this manuscript and for generally providing a sympathetic if captive audience. In addition, I should like to thank June Sochen of Northeastern Illinois University for generously sharing her thoughts on the meaning of the women's movement in the United States. My other intellectual debts are numerous, and should be evident both throughout the text and in the Suggested Readings that follow each chapter. (These readings should be taken as mere guides or signposts for the introductory student of American history for whom this book is intended.)

Finally, I am indebted to my family, particularly my wife, Sally, for their patience and encouragement without which nothing much gets accomplished in our household. As the dedication says, this book is for my children, Joseph Anthony and Joy Christina, so that they may know better the world they inherit.

Joseph M. Siracusa

1

Mr. Truman Takes Command

By the spring of 1945, Western forces had liberated France and pushed across the Rhine in a final drive into the heart of the German Third Reich. In a parallel development the Soviet Red Army began a last offensive within thirty miles of Berlin. Anticipating the political value that would accrue to the conqueror of the Nazi capital, the British, led by Prime Minister Winston Churchill, sought to launch a quick drive to reach Berlin first but were over-ruled on military grounds by General Dwight Eisenhower and the American government. Guided by the more calculating hand of Soviet leader Marshal Joseph Stalin, the Red Army liberated all the ancient capitals of central Europe, including Prague, Vienna, and Budapest. The American decision to hold back was probably a mistake, the full implications of which became clear only after the war. In any case, by the second week of April, the Americans had reached the Elbe River just sixty-three miles from Berlin, while the Soviets prepared for the final assault.

The sudden death of President Franklin Roosevelt from a massive cere-bral hemorrhage on April 12, 1945, came at this fateful moment in the war. The departure of Roosevelt on the eighty-third day of his unprecedented fourth term in office cast a pall over the leaders and peoples of the United Na-tions. The feeling of loss was intense. The British *Economist* summed it up this way: "It would be difficult to find hyperbole strong enough to exag-gerate the sense of loss felt all over the free world at the sudden news of President Roosevelt's death. Never before in a statesman of another

country and rarely for one of our own leaders have the outward pomp of cere-
monial mourning and also the inward and personal lamentation of the public
been more universal and heartfelt." Much the same was said in the Soviet
Union where, according to the Moscow correspondent of *The Times* of London, "President Roosevelt has been the personification of enlightened
American liberalism."

When Roosevelt died, the United States armed forces magazine, *Yank*,
observed without exaggeration that FDR had been commander in chief not
only of the armed forces but also of a whole generation. He was the only
president younger Americans had ever known; his New Deal legislation,
with its clear humanitarian spirit of government, was the only political program they had experienced. During World War I, the Federal Government
was still a comparatively small enterprise; by the time that Roosevelt
died, it touched in one way or another almost every facet of American
life. The question of government intervention in the American economy
to promote the welfare of the people—the hallmark of the New Deal—had
become settled. Equally significant, FDR gradually broke down the nation's interwar isolationist psychology and prepared for the nation's participation in World War II. Pearl Harbor, together with the president's
diplomacy, made certain that things would never be the same again. All in
all, to contemplate the career of Franklin Roosevelt was to come to grips
with the very problem of "great men" in history, whether or not one liked
the man.

The mantle of American leadership fell upon the shoulders of Harry S.
Truman, the seventh vice-president to succeed to the presidency upon the
death of the chief executive. Not unlike many other leaders of the nation,
President Truman rose to his position from humble beginnings. Born in
Lamar, Missouri, on May 8, 1884, the thirty-third president of the United
States was educated in the public school system, operated the family farm
near Independence, Missouri, and served in World War I, seeing action in
France. Studying law at night for two years in the early 1920s, Truman became involved in county government through the backing of Kansas City
political "Boss" Tom Pendergast.

Though elected to the United States Senate in 1934, it was not until
America entered World War II that Truman truly distinguished himself,
reaching national prominence as chairman of the Senate Committee to Investigate the National Defense Program. During his chairmanship of the Senate's war investigating committee, Truman was voted by Washington cor-
respondents, according to the *New York Times*, "as the civilian who, next to
President Roosevelt, 'knew most about the war.'" From his Senate position

and because of his record, Truman became the eventual compromise candidate for the vice-presidency at the Democratic convention in Chicago in 1944 in the bitter conflict between Harry A. Wallace, vice-president in FDR's third term and the undisputed choice of party radicals, and James F. Byrnes, director of war mobilization and reconversion, the almost undisputed choice of the conservatives.

In sharp contrast to the image of Truman held by his contemporaries as a man with a strong capacity for national leadership, scholars of all political persuasions have usually portrayed him as generally uninformed about his predecessor's foreign policies and as forced to rely heavily on Roosevelt's political and military advisers. To some extent this was so. For example, FDR had utterly failed to bring him into the larger picture of the internal workings of the Grand Alliance as well as to inform him of the atomic bomb project; but, then, Roosevelt had always acted as his own Secretary of State in alliance matters.

Still, for all his putative limitations, Truman was a man of his times, an avowed internationalist and an accomplished politician. Though acutely aware that, in his own words, "No man could possibly fill the tremendous void left by the passing of that noble soul [FDR]," the new occupant of the White House soon showed qualities of considerable executive ability, and was fully determined to be president in his own right, wholly responsible for the decisions that would have to be made. Like Roosevelt, Truman too would learn the art of managing the unmanageable.

During the transition of power in Washington, Germany collapsed under Allied hammer blows. As Soviet shells fell into Berlin, Adolf Hitler committed suicide on April 30, 1945, his body cremated in the garden by loyal followers. Facing the inevitable, German armies surrendered unconditionally at Reims on May 7–8. The Third Reich, which was supposed to last a thousand years, was finished.

President Truman initially adhered to Roosevelt's policy of collaboration with the Soviet Union, though evidence today suggests that FDR was having second thoughts about how best to deal with Stalin. Truman, like his advisers, came to recognize that Moscow viewed conciliatory gestures as a sign of weakness. The composition of the government of the reemerging Polish state continued to remain the great stumbling block, symbolizing in Western eyes Stalin's determination to have his own way throughout eastern Europe and elsewhere.

By the time Vyacheslav Molotov, the people's commissar for foreign affairs, arrived for talks in Washington in April 1945 en route to the founding conference of the United Nations to be held in San Francisco, Truman had served notice, to cite one account of the shift in mood, "that our agreements with the Soviet Union so far had been a one-way street and that could not continue: it was now or never." In their celebrated meeting of April 23, the president rebuked Molotov for Soviet behavior, all in the roughest Missouri language; the Soviet foreign minister, a dour, humorless man, defended his nation's interpretation of the Polish accord worked out at Yalta in February, adding that he had never been spoken to in such terms. According to Truman's interpreter, Charles Bohlen, these were "probably the first sharp words uttered during the war by an American President to a high Soviet official," although it is hard to imagine this particular aide of Joseph Stalin having escaped similar language at home.

On May 11, 1945, following the Nazi collapse, Truman ordered a sharp cutback in lend-lease shipments, including those to Russia; unfortunately, subordinates enforced the directive even more narrowly than the president probably intended, recalling Russian-bound ships at sea. Lend-lease to the USSR had previously been on a special basis—no information requested, no conditions of any kind—and apparently the president meant to send a signal to the Kremlin indicating a change in attitude. Stalin professed to be deeply pained and offended by the order, though the episode was soon smoothed over.

The Potsdam Conference

The way was then cleared for the last of the wartime summit conferences—code-named "Terminal"—held at Potsdam, near Berlin, from July 17 to August 2, 1945. Churchill was replaced midway through the conference by Clement Atlee whose Labour party had won the recent general election. The Allies (excluding the USSR on Japanese matters) agreed upon a last warning to Tokyo to surrender and agreed to establish a Council of Foreign Ministers to prepare treaties for Italy and the lesser Axis states, i.e., Rumania, Hungary, Bulgaria, and Finland. Moreover, the Big Three reaffirmed the policy of a joint occupation of vanquished Germany with fixed, zoned boundaries. The vexing problem of reparations was also tentatively settled.

According to the compromise reached, each occupying force would obtain its share of reparations from its own zone, with the Soviet Union to be compensated for its greater losses by 25 percent of the capital goods located within the western industrialized zones, a part of which would in turn be exchanged for food shipments from the largely agricultural areas occupied by the Soviet element. Moreover, the occupying forces were to embark on an overall program designed to denazify, decentralize, disarm, and democratize Germany until such time as it was deemed fit to rejoin the family of nations. Finally, Stalin, who was still technically at peace with Tokyo, agreed to enter into the war against Japan on August 15, making good a pledge given earlier that the Soviet Union would do so three months after the war in Europe had been concluded.

Potsdam, like the Yalta Conference before it, ended on a note of apparent friendship and continued cooperation. Truman's diary makes it clear that Stalin greatly impressed the president: "He (Stalin) is honest—but smart as hell." Still, Truman and the American planners were much less optimistic than their public remarks indicated. Soviet leaders had clearly revealed the unilateral nature of their concept of cooperation and their own plans for the future of eastern Europe. Many years later Truman recalled:

I hardly ever look back for the purpose of contemplating 'what might have been': Potsdam brings to mind 'what might have been' . . . . Certainly . . . Russia had no program except to take over the free part of Europe, kill as many Germans as possible, and fool the Western Alliance. Britain only wanted to control the Eastern Mediterranean, keep India, oil in Persia, the Suez Canal, and whatever else was floating loose.

There was an innocent idealist at one corner of that Round Table who wanted free waterways, Danube-Rhine-Kiel Canal, Suez, Black Sea Straits, Panama all free, a restoration of Germany, France, Italy, Poland, Czechslovakia, Rumania, and the Balkans, and a proper treatment of Latvia, Lithuania, Finland, free Phillipines, Indonesia, Indo-China, a Chinese Republic, and a free Japan.

What a show that was! But a large number of agreements were reached in spite of the set up—only to be broken as soon as the unconscionable Russian Dictator returned to Moscow! And I liked the little son of a bitch. . . .

The shape of the Cold War loomed ahead by the closing days of World War II.

Japan Collapses in the Pacific

Long-range B-29 bombers from Guam and other island bases had begun to rain destruction upon Japan by the close of 1944, culminating the next year in the greatest air offensive in history. All in all, approximately 160,000 tons of bombs were dropped upon Japan toward the end of the war, including firebomb raids that destroyed the center of Tokyo and other large Japanese cities. These raids alone killed 333,000 Japanese and wounded an additional 500,000 more. Air raids by July 1945 had, then, all but smashed the Japanese war economy.

Although elements within Japan long recognized they had lost the war and were prepared to sue for peace, the American government, still committed to a policy of unconditional surrender, was not inclined to bargain with them. Truman's warning to the Japanese issued at Potsdam to surrender or face total destruction still stood. The Japanese government and the Emperor favored making peace, but the militarists, led by the army, resisted. No less than one million American and Allied casualties were estimated by the Joint Chiefs of Staff to be the cost of invading the home islands.

Faced with this prospect, Truman and his advisers determined to use the atomic bomb against Japan in order to end the war as quickly as possible, assuming, of course, the final product of the multibillion dollar Manhattan Project lived up to expectations. On the morning of August 6, 1945, shortly after 8:15 AM, a lone B-29 bomber six miles up dropped the first atomic bomb on Hiroshima (population 350,000), the second most important military center in Japan, killing 140,000 people on the day of the attack and in the weeks immediately after it. The first atomic bomb to be used possessed the equivalent of only 12,500 tons of TNT—puny and primitive by current thermonuclear standards. Still, in that one terrible moment 60 percent of Hiroshima, an area equal to one-eighth of Manhattan, was destroyed. Three days later a second, slightly larger, atomic bomb was dropped on the city of Nagasaki, an important industrial and shipping area with a population of 253,000, of whom 70,000 were ultimately killed. The second atomic bomb possessed more power than 20,000 tons of TNT, a destructive force equivalent to the collective load of 4,000 B-29 bombers, or more than 2,000 times the blast power of what previously had been the world's most devastating bomb, the British "Grand Slam."

Though it was not admitted at the time, many residents of both cities would consequently succumb to radiation sickness; there were patients who had not been wounded but were wasting away. Japanese doctors were at a loss to explain it. In the United States there was a mixed reaction: "There was," according to one account, "an element of elation in the realization that we had perfected this devastating weapon for employment against an enemy who started the war and has told us he would rather be destroyed than surrender . . . (yet) there was sobering awareness of the tremendous responsibility involved." A turning point in the history of the contemporary world had been reached.

Meanwhile, reluctant to miss out on the kill, the Soviet Union declared war on Japan on August 8, a week sooner than the deadline of the pledge Stalin gave Truman at Potsdam. Nine minutes after its declaration, the Soviet Union's Far Eastern Army and Air Force attacked Japanese troops along the eastern Soviet-Manchuria borderlands. Yielding to the reality of the situation, the Emperor, supported by civilian advisers, finally overcame the Japanese militarists and ordered a surrender on August 14. For its part, the United States agreed to retain the institution of the Emperor system, stripped of pretension to divinity and subject to American occupation headed by General Douglas MacArthur. On September 2, a great Allied fleet sailed into Tokyo Bay for the formal surrender ceremony which took place on board the U.S.S. *Missouri*. World War II was thus brought to a close.

Controlling the Atom

The introduction of atomic weaponry into the American arsenal together with the implied peacetime use of the atom posed a number of serious problems for the Truman administration. Fully recognizing the revolutionary character of harnessing atomic energy, though perhaps underestimating the relative ability of other nations to translate their theoretical knowledge into practical application—for some, a deadly illusion—President Truman approached his task from the domestic and the international level. At the domestic level he requested Congress in October 1945 to enact legislation aimed at the creation of an Atomic Energy Commission "for the control, use and development of atomic energy within the United States."

At the international level, Truman met in Washington in November with British Prime Minister Atlee and his Canadian counterpart, Mackenzie King, and agreed on the need for action under United Nations auspices to outlaw atomic weapons, to ensure the use of atomic energy for peaceful purposes only, and to provide for inspection safeguards. To facilitate such action the foreign ministers of the Big Three, meeting in Moscow in December, consented to co-sponsor a resolution in the United Nations General Assembly establishing a United Nations Atomic Energy Commission. This was done on January 24, 1946.

To prepare American strategy, Secretary of State Byrnes appointed a special committee chaired by his under secretary of state, Dean G. Acheson, aided by a board of consultants headed by David Lilienthal, the chairman of the Tennessee Valley Authority and later the first chairman of the United States Atomic Energy Commission. The result, the Acheson-Lilienthal Report, made public on March 28,1946, concluded that the only way to ensure that nuclear energy could not be used for weapons was to create an international authority that would hold a monopoly over nuclear research and development. To this end, the report proposed a supranational International Atomic Development Authority, to be entrusted with all phases of the development and use of atomic energy, having the power to manage, control, inspect, and license all related activities. What the proposed agency would not have was authority to apply sanctions against wrongdoers. Truman chose Bernard Baruch, a financier and longtime Democrat, to present the plan to the United Nations' Atomic Energy Commission in June.

The Baruch Plan, as it soon became known, proposed the cessation of the manufacture of atomic bombs, the disposal of existing American bombs, and the creation of the international authority recommended in the Acheson-Lilienthal Report. More important, Baruch's plan provided for sanctions not subject to the veto of any permanent member of the United Nations Security Council and insisted that an adequate system of control and inspection be in effect *before* the United States handed over control of its nuclear facilities.

Moscow's response came five days later in an address delivered by the Soviet United Nations Representative, Andrei Gromyko. To no one's surprise, the Soviet Union rejected the American proposal, calling simply for the prohibition of the production and use of nuclear weapons, and for the destruction of existing stockpiles while providing for no serious inspection scheme to monitor compliance. The Soviet counterproposal was, in turn, rejected by the United States. Moscow's principal motive in rebuffing the American proposal derived from fear that the Baruch Plan would subject the Soviet economy to outside interference, not to mention waiving the Soviet right to veto in the case of punishment. Furthermore, any effective inspection system would necessarily mean a breach of the Iron Curtain, and this Premier Stalin refused to tolerate. Both sides agreeing only to disagree, the proceedings were adjourned indefinitely on March 30, 1948.

To the Truman Doctrine and the Marshall Plan

Upon his return from Potsdam, President Truman continued publicly to emphasize Allied unity. Like Roosevelt before him, Truman said he found it easy to get along with Stalin. Furthermore, declared the president to the American people in August 1945, "there was a fundamental accord and agreement upon the objectives ahead of us"—an assertion that hardly reflected the deep-seated Soviet-American differences over such matters as reparations and occupation policies in Germany and Austria. While relations between the Allies appeared tranquil enough on the surface, policy makers at the highest levels had moved well in the direction of locating and identifying the Soviet Union as the most serious threat to international peace.

On October 5, 1945, in a radio broadcast originating from Washington, Secretary of State Byrnes announced to the nation that the first session of the council of foreign ministers, which had met in London in September, closed in stalemate. The tensions that had undermined Allied diplomacy in the closing stages of World War II now threatened to surface. The London conference broke up mainly over the unexpected Soviet refusal to allow China and France to participate in the drafting of peace treaties with Italy and the lesser Axis nations, the objection being that only nations signatory to surrender documents had the right to speak on the subject at this time.

Other difficulties included the joint Anglo-American refusal to recognize the pro-Soviet governments of Bulgaria and Rumania. The Americans based their refusal squarely on the gound that freedom of speech and assembly were still being denied to the Bulgarian and Rumanian people, basic rights without which political self-determination could not be realized. Draft treaties for Italy, Rumania, Hungary, Bulgaria, and Finland were finally arranged by the time a peace conference of twenty-one nations assembled in Paris in July 1946. They were signed and went into effect on February 10, 1947, but not before the Cold War rivalry that would animate Soviet-American relations for the next generation and beyond had taken root.

Despite late efforts to assuage Soviet fears, and in a manner that foreshadowed the administration's hardening attitude toward Stalin in the wake of the fruitless second meeting of the Council of Foreign Ministers, the United States State Department vigorously continued to object to the Soviet establishment of totalitarian political regimes and economic control over the countries of eastern and central Europe. In full conformity with the American position of self-determination and equality of commerical opportunity, State Department planners argued that America should use its great influence to break the Soviet grip. The method chosen to resist the Soviets lay principally in the economic sphere—a natural choice, given the dominance of the American economy in the postwar period.

Specifically, through the granting of credits, the United States hoped to encourage more political independence for nations behind the Iron Curtain—countries east of the line from Stettin in the Baltic to Trieste in the Adriatic—to use Churchill's famous allusion. At the same time, the United States hoped to persuade the Kremlin to loosen its grip over the same countries. With the proverbial battle line drawn, the Truman administration began to abandon hope of accommodating Stalin's fears and plans for expansion by early 1946. "I'm tired of babying the Soviets," President Truman was alleged to have told his secretary of state.

For their part, Soviet leaders began the difficult task of preparing the Russian people for the struggle ahead, for the continued sacrifices they would have to make in the name of rebuilding their war-torn economy, and for the inevitable postponement of the production of consumer goods in favor of heavy industry. To achieve their goal the Communist party of the Soviet Union appealed to the heightened sense of Russian nationalism that accompanied the Red Army's victory over nazi Germany and Japan and to the Marxist theme of capitalist antagonism to industrial socialism. The most significant appeal was that made by Stalin on February 9, 1946. In a speech regarded by some as the single most important Soviet pronouncement of the immediate postwar world, Stalin revived international class conflict in a way that suggested that the USSR was clearly a revolutionary power. In a characteristic reaction, H. Freeman Matthews, the State Department's director of the office of European affairs, noted that Stalin's speech constituted, "the most important and authoritative guide to postwar Soviet policy."

In the so-called Long Telegram of February 22, 1946, a response to a State Department request for an interpretive analysis of the significance and meaning of Stalin's and other related pronouncements, the American chargé in Moscow, George F. Kennan, formulated an assessment of Soviet foreign policy that uniquely captured the mood of the Truman administration's determination to resist the perceived threat of Stalinist Russia to world peace. Not only was Kennan able to explain the basis of Soviet foreign policy, he also had a remedy: containment. What "we have here," argued Kennan persuasively, is "a political force committed fanatically to the belief that with the [United States] there can be no permanent *modus vivendi*, that it is desirable and necessary that the internal harmony of our society be disrupted, our traditional way of life be destroyed, the international authority of our state be broken, if Soviet power is to be secure."

What to do about it was compounded by the fact that Soviet leadership was "seemingly inaccessible to consideration of reality in its basic reaction," though not in the same sense that informed Hitler's reckless ambitions. "Impervious to logic of reason," concluded Kennan, "it [USSR] is highly sensitive to the logic of force. For this reason it can easily withdraw— and usually does—when strong resistance is encountered at any point." Kennan became permanently and unwittingly identified with this policy in his famous "X" article published in the influential journal, *Foreign Affairs,* in 1947. At that time he refined what has since become the classic definition of containment: "Soviet pressure against the free institutions of the western world is something that can be contained by the adroit and vigilant application of counterforce at a series of constantly shifting geographical and political points, corresponding to the shifts and maneuvers of Soviet policy, but which cannot be charmed out of existence." On November 24, 1948, the doctrine of containment was officially adopted by the Truman administration.

Throughout 1946 Soviet actions tended to confirm the administration's worst fears. While pursuing obstructionist policies in the occupation control councils in Germany and Austria, the Soviets continued to retain forces in Manchuria and northern Iran, in the latter area preventing government troops from intervening against communist-organized rebels in the province of Azerbaijan. In March 1946 Iran protested to the United Nations Security Council, demanding the evacuation of the Red Army from the disputed territory. By early May Soviet troop withdrawal had been completed but not before the United Nations had showed its powerlessness in the face of the Kremlin's veto power.

The United States learned the lesson that the USSR could only be checked by policies initiated by itself. Accordingly, the Truman administration was determined to resist what it regarded as Soviet aggression the next time it reared its head, although the actual form and timing of that resistance were much in doubt. The immediate background of the pronouncement of the Truman Doctrine was the official disclosure in February 1947 that the British government would shortly be terminating its military and economic support of the existing Greek and Turkish regimes. The president's response both to the plight of the British and to the deteriorating situation in Greece and Turkey was swift and unequivocal. Requesting urgent economic and financial assistance for the relief of these countries, Truman declared to a joint session of Congress on March 12, 1947: "I believe that it must be the policy of the United States to support free peoples who are resisting attempted subjugation by armed minorities or by outside pressures. I believe that we must assist free peoples to work out their own destinies in their own way." The exact meaning of these words, although Truman specifically qualified them to mean "that our help should be primarily through economic and financial aid," has been the subject of much historical debate.

Whatever the president meant, there can be little doubt that his speech was a major turning point in modern American foreign policy. Significantly, this was a policy that had the support of Republicans and Democrats alike, the former organized under the direction of Senator Arthur Vandenberg of Michigan, the leading Republican spokesman on foreign policy in the Senate and one of the earliest supporters of a bipartisan approach to postwar international relations. The only element left to argue about was tactics.

By late May 1947 it had become alarmingly apparent that the Truman administration had grossly underestimated the destruction of the European economy in the aftermath of World War II. "Europe is steadily deteriorating," observed Under Secretary of State William L. Clayton; furthermore, "the political position reflects the economic." As the fate and well-being of the United States were invariably bound up with the fate and well-being of Western Europe, it was probably only natural that Washington would seek to repair the fortunes of its natural allies.

During commencement exercises at Harvard University on June 5, 1947, the eminent soldier and secretary of state, George C. Marshall, observed that in the name of enlightened self-interest, "It is logical that the United States should do whatever it is able to do to assist in the return of normal economic health in the world, without which there can be no political stability and no assured peace." Marshall called for the reconstruction of Europe by Europeans, and so was born the Marshall Plan or, more accurately, the European Recovery Program, signed into law by President Truman on April 3, 1948. Two weeks later the sixteen Western European nations involved met in Paris to set up the necessary machinery for economic cooperation—the Organization for European Economic Cooperation. From that time until the Marshall Plan officially came to an end on December 31, 1951, the United States pumped $13 billion into the economy of Western Europe.

From War to Peace at Home

The demands of World War II wrought profound changes in the American economy as well as in the American people. As war approached in the last months of 1941, army spending hit $2 billion a month; in the first six months of 1942, military spending was $100 billion. In 1939 the Federal budget was $9 billion; by 1945 it was $166 billion. The war created seventeen million new jobs. Production soared so high that Americans knew no serious deprivations. Overnight, the unemployment of the depression had been wiped out; in fact, the labor market significantly increased. Women and blacks entered the industrial marketplace on a scale previously unknown. The working mother was one aspect of the story. So, too, were the thousands of blacks who migrated from the rural South to the industrial plants of the North. Everyone worked compulsory overtime.

What were people to do with this new found affluence? Consumer goods were often not available, but by 1943 firms were advertising all kinds of products. All cashed in on wartime sentiment, and the result was more often than not regrettable. Tourism within the nation flourished. "Miami's pledge to America at War" was a holiday in the sun—at expense-account prices. Western Electric, the production subsidiary of the Bell Telephone System, reminded people that, "in a world free of dictators . . . the telephone will help to place all peoples . . . on friendly speaking terms." And in the month of the D-day landing, a confident General Electric Company announced: "Now—we'll be glad to put your name down for earliest available data on postwar air conditioning and refrigerator equipment."

It was a time for enterprise. In 1941 Coca-Cola was the most widely available consumer item in the United States, and the company's president, Robert W. Woodruff, was determined to maintain its position. He did so and thereby guaranteed that Coke would become the world's number one drink. He somehow persuaded the armed forces that Coke was essential to armed forces personnel. The company gained access to armed forces sugar supplies (not available on the open market) and Coca-Cola manufacturing equipment got priority shipping along with military hardware and supplies.

Equally remarkable perhaps was the story of Wrigley's chewing gum, advertised after 1941 as "a war material." Gum was half sugar, but also required tree sap from areas occupied by the Japanese. Wrigley convinced the army that chewing gum relieved tension, helped clean teeth, and was a substitute for smoking in cases where cigarettes were dangerous or unavailable. He also obtained vital space for his product on military ships returning from South America (an alternative source of raw materials) and access to government sugar stocks.

The hucksters also had their day, but more was involved here than Madison Avenue dreaming. During the war new products evolved—hi-fi, TV, dishwasher, etc.—which were to revolutionize the lifestyle of the 1950s. The promise of a better material world ahead was not an empty one.

In terms of wartime finance, by mid-1943 World War II was costing $8 billion per month—the equivalent of the yearly New Deal budgets of the past. By the time of the Japanese surrender, the national debt had risen from $48 billion in 1941 to $247 billion. Taxes raised an estimated 40 percent of the total costs of the war, $350 billion; the remainder was met by the time-honored method of borrowing. Millions of Americans were encouraged to invest in war bonds. Through the introduction of the payroll income deduction scheme proposed by Beardsley Ruml, chairman of the Federal Reserve Bank of New York, the war years witnessed a veritable tax revolution, with the number of Americans paying income taxes increasing from four million in 1939 to approximately fifty million by 1945.

Less than a week after the Japanese surrender, President Truman delivered a special message to Congress presenting a twenty-one-point program for the reconstruction period ahead. With no illusions that the process of reconversion would be an easy one, the president outlined a number of policies that would govern the transition of American society from war to peace: demobilizing the armed forces as soon as possible, cancelling and settling war contracts, clearing war plants to make way for peacetime production, holding the line on prices and rents until fair competition could be restored to prevent inflation and undue hardship on consumers, keeping wages in line so that their increase would not precipitate price rises, removing all possible wartime government controls with a view to facilitating reconversion and expansion while retaining only those that were deemed absolutely necessary, and preventing rapid decrease of wages or purchasing power. Among other things the special message signaled the inevitable return of politics to the domestic front. Put succinctly by the *New York Times,* "Some Democrats saw in it [the president's message] a great state document; others viewed it as a belated recognition of Congress as a co-equal branch of the government. Republican spokesmen found in it a continuation of the New Deal and a sign that the Truman Administration had decided to go to the left."

The demobilization of the armed forces proved no real difficulty. By the spring of 1946, seven million servicemen, not to mention large numbers of servicewomen not subject to the Selective Services Act, had returned home, determined to pick up where they had left off. To cushion the return to civilian life, numerous laws were enacted that provided, among other things, job recruitment, unemployment pay, insurance, home loans, and educational opportunities. The latter category alone allowed twelve million veterans access to technical and university education. By 1947 more than four million Americans were taking advantage of the Servicemen's Readjustment Act, the so-called G.I. Bill of Rights.

For all its popularity among veterans, the quick reduction of the armed forces' strength alarmed some civilian and military planners charged with national security planning. It was probably at this time that America's possession of the atomic bomb began to become a substitute for thinking about responding to conventional attacks with conventional forces. In any case, the Selective Service Act, which had governed the induction of over ten million servicemen since 1940, expired on March 31, 1947, though provisions were made for the maintenance of records and conscription in emergency situations.

Congress also complied with the president's request for early action on a full employment bill. The Employment Act of 1946 required the chief executive to submit an annual economic report, established a council of economic adivsers to bring wisdom to presidential economics, and declared the intention of the Federal government to promote maximum employment, production, and purchasing power. Though it did not specifically endorse the economics of John Maynard Keynes, the act clearly foreshadowed policies of deficit spending and unbalanced budgets. In other areas a spate of wartime agencies was abolished by executive order.

Between September 1945 and January 1946, $35 billion in contracts were cancelled, and hundreds of war plants, previously owned by the government were sold off, mainly to the corporations that had been running them. Within this time more than 90 percent of the war plants had been reconverted to peacetime uses, bringing high employment and prosperity. The specter of another Great Depression, with estimates of as many as eight million unemployed, never materialized. Controlling inflation was another matter. Americans emerged from the war with unprecedented savings of approximately $145 billion, which they were determined to spend on homes, automobiles, and the many gadgets that the American people regarded as their birthright.

To curb wartime inflation, the movement of prices, wages, and rents came under the control of the Office of Price Administration (OPA) in 1942. General prices had already risen 25 percent by then, but the line was held thereafter. By mid-1946 business, labor, and farmers clamored for the end of these controls so that each could claim a bit more of the American economic pie. Trying to balance the continuing prospect of prosperity with the duty to curb inflationary pressure, the president vetoed a much-amended follow-on version of OPA in the hope that a compromise might yet be worked out.

For twenty-five days the prices of commodities and residential rents were allowed to find their own levels, while political passions ran high. The chairman of the Republican National Committee, Carroll Reece, summed up the feeling of the opposition: "Having long since lost all semblance of control over the Congress in which his party has majorities in both houses, the President now, apparently, lost control of himself."

On July 25, the president reluctantly signed a measure revalidating the OPA, with specified exemptions; in the interim, prices jumped 25 percent and threatened to go even higher. In November, shortly after the election of the 80th Congress, Truman abandoned all price, wage, and salary controls, with the exception of ceilings on rents and sugar. "In one swoop," noted one observer, "the President virtually cut the American economy loose from the shaky moorings of a four-year-old stabilization program." Now it was labor's turn.

Within weeks of V-J day, a half-million American workers went on strike; by the end of the year, strikes had disrupted the production of steel and automobiles. The auto workers finally settled in March 1946 for a wage increase of 18.5 percent. More ominously, John L. Lewis led the country's 400,000 soft coal miners out of the pits at 12:01 AM on April 1 over a series of deadlocked issues involving health and welfare programs and wages. Truman in turn seized the mines, retaining control when the bituminous operators failed to accept a contract that the United Mine Workers had negotiated under Federal auspices. A second strike called by Lewis in late November in defiance of a court order resulted in his being held in contempt of court at the Federal level. He was personally fined $10,000, and the UMW was fined $3,500,000, later reduced to $70,000. The miners returned to work in early December, having won most of their demands. Earlier in May, Truman, angry about the disruption the strikes were causing the economy and himself, had gone before Congress to seek authority to draft striking rail workers into the army. The railroad strike, which had paralyzed America's commerce and marooned 90,000 passengers, was settled on the president's terms within forty-eight hours.

Complaints of inflation, together with antiunion sentiment, translated themselves into a conservative Republican victory in the midterm congressional elections of 1946. With a gain of thirteen seats in the Senate and fifty-six seats in the House, the GOP controlled the Congress for the first time in fourteen years. The 80th Congress, led by Republicans and conservative southern Democrats, managed to antagonize farmers, westerners, and ethnic groups. Most significantly, Congress managed to antagonize unionists to the point where labor gladly reembraced the president, whose previous calls for the seizing of coal mines and railroads were forgiven if not forgotten.

In a determined effort to put labor in its place, Congress passed the Taft-Hartley Act on June 23, 1947, over Truman's veto. Among other things, the new law banned the closed shop, which had prohibited the hiring of nonunion workers; allowed employers to sue unions either for broken contracts or damages resulting from strikes; established a Federal Mediation and Conciliation Service; required employers to submit a sixty-day notice or "cooling off" period in termination of contract; authorized the Federal government to obtain injunctions imposing a cooling off period of eighty days on strikes threatening the national well-being; mandated that unions make public their financial statements; prohibited union contributions to political campaigns; and allowed union officials to take an oath that they were not members of the Communist party.

Truman remonstrated in his veto that this particular piece of legislation reversed the basic direction of the nation's labor policy, injected the government into private economic affairs on an unprecedented scale, and conflicted with important principles of a democratic society. Moreover, he concluded,"its provisions would cause more strikes, not fewer." With the return of labor to the Democratic fold in 1948, one of the firs⁺ electoral victims of the Taft-Hartley Act was Representative Fred Hartley, Jr. of Minnesota.

If the 80th Congress was in no mood to help labor, neither was it in the mood to help the nation's blacks. For reasons of their own, Republicans and southern Democrats joined forces to block civil rights legislation of any kind. Prompted by protests against the outbreak of racial murders in the South in 1946, which included the cold-blooded murder of two young blacks and their wives by an unmasked band of twenty whites at Monroe, Georgia, the president appointed a special Committee on Civil Rights in July. After ten months of deliberation, the committee, headed by Charles E. Wilson, president of General Electric Company, issued its report entitled "To Secure These Rights." "The pervasive gap between our aims and what we actually do," suggested the report, "is creating a kind of moral dry rot which eats away at the emotional and rational bases of democratic belief." On February 2, 1948, Truman requested Congress to implement the report's recommendations, including legislation to outlaw lynching and Jim Crow practices while establishing a nationwide system for monitoring civil liberties.

In the face of Republican-controlled Congress and in the full knowledge that he would alienate many southern Democrats, the president in July 1948 issued Executive Order 9981 barring segregation in the armed forces— really, a reflection of the impact of World War II on the area of civil rights. In 1949 a Federal law further barred discrimination in Federal civil service positions. It was in these years also that the great Brooklyn Dodger second baseman Jackie Robinson broke the color barrier in major league sports.

The 80th Congress moved more positively in the sphere of governmental reorganization. The Presidential Succession Act of 1947 revised the law of 1886, making the speaker of the House of Representatives first and the president pro tempore of the Senate second in line of succession behind the president and vice-president, followed by the secretary of state and other cabinet members according to rank. The year 1947 also witnessed the inception of the Twenty-Second Amendment to the Constitution—essentially an anti-Roosevelt gesture limiting the president to no more than two terms in office—as well as the establishment of the Commission on the Organization of the Executive Branch of the government under the direction of former president Herbert Hoover. (The amendment was ratified on February 26, 1951.)

The final report of the commission proved extremely influential: almost two hundred of the report's recommendations were fully or partially accepted. In late July 1947, President Truman signed legislation for the unification of the armed forces and named James Forrestal, then secretary of the navy, as the secretary of defense, with cabinet status. The act further established the National Security Council and under it the Central Intelligence Agency, which was to correlate and evaluate intelligence activity relating to the nation's security.

The 1948 Election

With the growing prospect of a GOP victory in the fall, the Republican National Convention meeting at Philadelphia in June 1948 nominated Thomas E. Dewey, the moderate-to-liberal governor of New York, on the third ballot. Dewey, who had polled 44.5 percent of the popular vote in 1944 against Franklin Roosevelt, gladly accepted his party's nomination, adding that he had come to the convention "unfettered by a single obligation or promise to any living person, free to join with you in selecting to serve our nation the finest men and women in the nation." As his running mate he chose the even-more-liberal Governor Earl Warren of California. Joining ranks with his erstwhile antagonists such as Senators Robert L. Taft of Ohio and Arthur H. Vandenberg, Dewey ran a subdued campaign.

The Democratic National Convention meeting in July, also at Philadelphia, was a different story. Truman was nominated by default, for lack of serious challengers. Senator Alben W. Barkley of Kentucky was Truman's selection for vice-president. Several southern delegations bolted the convention in protest against the strong civil rights plank, and shortly afterward nominated Governor J. Strom Thurmond of South Carolina to run for president on a States' Rights or Dixiecrat ticket. To make matters worse, the disgruntled followers of the controversial Henry Wallace, secretary of commerce, who had been dropped from Truman's cabinet in September 1946 for challenging the president's get-tough policy with the Soviets, organized the Progressive party to run for the presidency. With the Democrats splintered and the Republicans united, the election of the confident Dewey seemed a foregone conclusion, if one could believe the pollsters and pundits. Truman, however, refused to play dead.

Truman literally took his campaign to the people, traveling 23,000 miles and making 272 speeches. In town after town, he made the performance of the "do-nothing, good-for-nothing" 80th Congress the target of his attack. His message was simple and unequivocal; Were the special privilege boys or the people going to run the country? "How far," he asked the voters in Springfield, Illinois, "do you suppose the real estate lobby would get with Abraham Lincoln?" On the eve of the election, Truman waited at his home in Independence, Missouri, persuaded that he had developed a hidden groundswell to carry him into the presidency on his own merits. To the surprise of everyone but himself, the president won handily, receiving a popular vote of 24,105,812 (52.8 percent) to Dewey's 21,970,065 (44.5 percent). The electoral victory was even more impressive at 303 to 189. Significantly, the Democrats regained control of the Senate and the House. Never had the political prophets been more perplexed.

The Fair Deal

Finally president in his own right, Truman sought both to extend and enlarge upon the New Deal legislation of his predecessor. In his State of the Union message to Congress broadcast nationally on January 5, 1949, the president announced that "every segment of our population and every individual has a right to expect from our Government a fair deal." Interpreting the presidential election of 1948 as a mandate from the people, he began, "We have rejected the discredited theory that the fortunes of the Nation should be in the hands of a privileged few. We have abandoned 'the trickle-down' concept of national prosperity." In its place, he said, "we believe that our economic system should rest on a democratic foundation and that wealth should be created for the benefit of all." Translated into specifics, the Fair Deal argued for a series of antiinflationary measures enacted at the national level; the repeal of the Taft-Hartley Act; more homes; higher corporate taxes; special attention to rural problems; the development of natural resources with a view to conservation; and raising the standard of living through social security, health, education, and civil rights.

The 81st Congress met the president halfway, enacting more liberal legislation than any Congress during the past ten years: it increased minimum wages from forty to seventy-five cents per hour; expanded social security benefits while extending coverage to ten million more people; expanded public welfare through rural electrification, soil conservation, and flood control developments; extended immigration quotas under the Displaced Persons Act; set up a National Science Foundation; provided for some slum clearance and low-cost housing; and granted the chief executive power to deal with inflation. In most other areas the Fair Deal ran into a stone wall. While some programs were deemed too costly, others, such as civil rights and national health insurance, encountered the resistance of southern Democrats and special interest groups, particularly the American Medical Association. There were other problems.

In response to recommendations made by the Presidential Commission on Employee Loyalty, established in November of 1946, Truman issued an executive order in March 1947 calling for an immediate investigation of the loyalty and intentions of every person entering civilian employment in any department or agency of the executive branch of the government. Those already holding positions were to be scrutinized by the Federal Bureau of Investigation, their fate resting essentially on the decision of their department heads' willingness to pledge personal responsibility for their subordinates. Done generally in moderation, the procedure passed over millions of employees, with only a few thousand closely examined. The final effort resulted in several hundred dismissals, mostly based on guilt by association.

Of course the real targets were communists and communist sympathizers. To parry accusations that his administration was "soft" on communism (mainly the repercussion of establishment support for former State Department employee Alger Hiss who was found guilty of perjury in 1948), Truman went a step further in January 1949 when the nation's leading twelve communists—later, eleven—were called to trial on charges of violating the Smith Act of 1940, making it a criminal offense to advocate the forceful overthrow of the government. Convicted, the eleven challenged the constitutionality of the Smith Act. In 1951, in *Dennis et al.* v. *U.S.*, the Supreme Court upheld the law, with Justices Hugo Black and William Douglas dissenting. In September 1950 Congress passed, over the President's veto, the McCarran Act, providing for, among other things, the registration of communists and communist-front organizations, as well as for the internment of communists during national emergencies.

In this atmosphere it was learned that Dr. Klaus Fuchs, a German-born scientist working for the British, had provided atomic secrets to the Soviets; furthermore, he implicated a number of Americans, including Julius and

Ethel Rosenberg, who had transmitted classified information to Moscow from 1942 to 1947. Both Rosenbergs were consequently executed. These events, together with the "loss of China"—the fall of China to the communists after the Chinese civil war—and news of the Soviet acquisition of an atomic bomb, gave extremists the opening they always seek in a time of troubles. One of these extremists was Joseph R. McCarthy, the Republican senator from Wisconsin. McCarthy declared in a speech at Wheeling, West Virginia, in early 1950 that 205 (later revised to 57) communists had infiltrated the State Department. Though McCarthy's accusations gained wide publicity, a special subcommittee of the Senate Foreign Relations Committee found the allegations to be baseless. In the midst of the national emergency proclaimed later in the year resulting from the outbreak of the Korean War, the senator's accusations increased while partisan attacks against the Truman administration were stepped up. Before McCarthyism would spend itself, incalculable damage would be done to the careers and lives of many innocent Americans. The loyalty oath soon replaced common sense.

Containment in Action

The repeated failure of the Council of Foreign Ministers to reach agreement on Germany by late 1947 led to moves by the Western powers toward the creation of a unified and self-governing West Germany. The Anglo-American elements had already taken one large step in that direction by the economic merging of their three zones. Consultations in London in the spring of 1948 resulted in agreements, announced June 7, proposing the creation of a West German government with some safeguards planned for the control of the Ruhr industries. The Germans of the Western zones would elect members of a constituent assembly, which in turn would draw up a constitution for a federal state that might eventually include the Eastern Zone.

Accordingly, the German Federal Republic was inaugurated at Bonn in September 1949. Military government terminated, although occupation forces remained. The Federal Republic was soon made eligible for Marshall Plan aid, and under its first chancellor, Konrad Adenauer, showed a spirit of willing cooperation with the West. For its part the Kremlin resolved to do everything possible to defeat the program of American "imperialism." Communist-inspired strikes in France and Italy sought in vain to deter these countries from accepting Marshall Plan aid. Treaties of defensive alliance linking the Soviet Union with Finland, Bulgaria, Hungary, and Rumania were added to treaties previously negotiated with Czechoslovakia, Poland, and Yugoslavia. And in February 1948 a communist coup overthrew the domocratic government of Czechoslovakia and installed one firmly attached to the Kremlin. This blow to the West was partly compensated for later in the year when Yugoslavia, under Marshal Tito, broke with Moscow.

Complaining that the Western powers (including France) had destroyed the four-power control over Germany, the Soviets set out to eject their erstwhile allies from Berlin, which lay wholly within the Soviet zone. Berlin, with no guaranteed surface corridor of communications with the West, had restrictions upon the movement of persons to and from the city imposed in April 1948 (followed in June by the prohibition of all surface transportation between Berlin and the Western Zone). The Western powers were faced with the prospect of withdrawing their garrisons from Berlin in defeat or of supplying not only them, but also the two million inhabitants of West Berlin. Despite the initial impression in some quarters that the Western forces might consider leaving the former German capitol if the suffering of the populace became too great, the Truman administration decided to act.

Rejecting advice that he open the road by military force, the president, in consultation with the British, resorted to air transport, the only means for which the West had signed agreements with the Soviets. The "airlift" not thought possible by some observers on the scene commenced at once, and, by September 1, American and British planes were flying in four thousand tons of supplies daily. Soviet planes occasionally threatened but never ventured to attack. Allied persistence and patience finally paid dividends as the Soviets ended the blockade in May 1949. Shortly afterward the Soviet-sponsored German Democratic Republic was called into existence. Like its competitor at Bonn, East Germany rested upon a constitution dedicated to the unification of all Germany. Unlike its competitor, it would not be allowed to deviate from the party line emanating from Moscow.

The communist coup in Czechoslovakia and the Berlin blockade greatly alarmed the Western powers. There was, after all, no guarantee that the Soviets, with their preponderant number of armed forces, might not renew efforts to oust the Western allies from Berlin or to strangle the German Federal Republic in its infancy. "Containment" of Soviet Russia, till now dependent mainly upon economic and political means, appeared in need of military backing. For if the USSR could be certain that an act of aggression against any one of the free nations of Western Europe would mean a conflict with the others and also with the United States, it might be deterred from such acts. Neither America's nuclear monopoly nor the United Nations Security Council, because of the Soviet veto, could supply such a deterrent. It was in this context that the West turned to Article 51 of the United Nations Charter, which legalized "collective self-defense" by groups within the United Nations. In the Americas, the Rio Pact of September 2, 1947, had already invoked Article 51 in a hemispheric collective-security agreement; in Europe a beginning had been made in March 1948 when Great Britain, France, and the Benelux countries signed at Brussels a fifty-year treaty of economic, social, and cultural collaboration and collective self-defense.

Support for the treaty was promptly proposed by President Truman in an address to Congress in March 1948. The president spoke frankly of the danger from Moscow, calling for the adoption of a universal military training program (which Congress defeated), and temporary reenactment of Selective Service legislation. The buildup of American armed forces strength, which had been allowed to disintegrate since 1945, began with the draft act of June 1948, requiring military service of men from nineteen to twenty-five years of age. With the aid of this, and under the stimulus of the Korean War, the combined strength of the American armed forces grew from 1,350,000 in 1948 to 3,630,000 in June 1952. The way for collective action was cleared when the Senate, in the Vandenberg Resolution of June 11, 1948, articulated the proposition that the United States should associate itself, "by constitutional processes, with such regional and other collective arrangements as are based on continuous and effective self-help and mutual aid, and as affect its national security."

The Vandenberg Resolution was the prelude to the North Atlantic Treaty (1949), a significant and profound venture in search of meaningful collective security. The treaty—a fundamental departure from the American principle of "no permanent alliances"—was signed by twelve nations of the northern Atlantic and western European areas, a number increased to fifteen in 1955 with the inclusion of West Germany. The parties agreed to settle all disputes peacefully among themselves and to develop their capacity to resist armed attack. But the heart of the treaty was Article 5 with its "Three Musketeers" pledge that an armed attack upon any one of the members in Europe or North America would be considered an attack upon all; furthermore, the treaty pledged each member to assist any attacked party "by such action as it deems necessary, including the use of armed forces." Thus originated the North Atlantic Treaty Organization, or NATO.

Two other events in 1949 also shaped the direction of the United States' defense effort. The first was the revelation in September that the USSR had exploded its first atomic bomb; the second was the completion of the communist conquest of all of mainland China, followed by the proclamation of the People's Republic of China at Peking in October. The latter event was regarded as a major triumph in the Kremlin's program of world revolution; the former, a potential mortal danger to the continental United States itself. One top-secret document, Policy Paper Number 68 of the National Security Council (or NSC 68), approved by President Truman in September 1950, went so far as to estimate, in the "period of peril" motif so often employed in modern times, "that within the next four years the U.S.S.R will attain the capability of seriously damaging vital centers of the United States, provided it strikes a first blow and provided further that the blow is opposed by no more effective opposition than we now have programmed." Though existing American retaliatory capability was adequate to deter the Soviets from launching a direct military attack, NSC 68 warned that the time was fast approaching when that power would not be sufficient.

Washington therefore had little choice but to increase both its atomic and (if feasible) its thermonuclear capabilities. The Soviet possession of atomic weapons, according to NSC 68, had the dual effect not only of putting a premium on a more violent and ruthless prosecution of the Kremlin's design for world conquest, but also of putting "a premium on piecemeal aggression against others, counting on our unwillingness to engage in atomic war unless we are directly attacked." To counter such an eventuality as well as to provide an argument for raising the Defense Department's budget of $13.5 billion, NSC 68 recommended a more rapid buildup of political, economic, and military strength than had been previously contemplated. Only such a program, concluded NSC 68, could "postpone and avert the disastrous situation which, in light of the Soviet Union's probable fission bomb capability and possible thermonuclear bomb capability, might arise in 1954 on a continuation of our present program." Acccordingly, "by acting promptly and vigorously in such a way that this date is, so to speak, pushed into the future, we could permit time for the process of accommodation, withdrawal, and frustration to produce the necessary changes in the Soviet system." The "selling" of NSC 68 to the American people came from unexpected quarters.

The North Koreans, on the morning of June 25, 1950 (Korean time), launched a well-organized attack along the entire width of the 38th parallel, the postwar dividing line between the Soviet-supported Democratic People's Republic of Korea and the American-supported Republic of Korea, or South Korea. Within a few hours of receiving the news, President Truman requested a meeting of the U.N. Security Council, and on the afternoon of June 25 (New York time), that body adopted a resolution, introduced by the United States, declaring the North Korean action a "breach of peace," demanding that the aggressor withdraw beyond the 38th parallel, and calling upon all members of the U.N. "to render every assistance to the United Nations in the execution of their resolution and to refrain from giving assistance to the North Korean authorities." Owing to the absence of the Soviet delegate (who had boycotted the U.N. because of its refusal to seat the representative of communist China in place of the member of the Taiwan regime), the resolution passed the Security Council by a vote of 9–0 (Yugoslavia not voting). On June 27 the Council recommended that U.N. members "furnish such assistance to the Republic of Korea as may be necessary to repel the armed attack and to restore international peace and security in the area." Two weeks later General Douglas MacArthur was named commander for all U.N. forces serving in Korea.

President Truman acted promptly in throwing the weight of America into the balance. On June 27 he announced that he had ordered United States air and sea forces to provide Korean government troops with cover and support. Three days later in Tokyo, the president authorized the use of American ground troops in Korea, ordered a naval blockade of the Korean coast, and directed the air force to attack targets in North Korea "wherever militarily necessary." In his announcement of June 27, President Truman also revealed other action that constituted a distinct change of policy: "Communism had passed beyond the use of subversion to conquer independent nations and will now use armed invasion and war." Under the circumstances, the president felt justified in accelerating military assistance to French forces fighting Ho Chi Minh's independence movement in Indochina and to the Philippines, as well as stretching the nation's "defensive perimeter" to include Taiwan, the refuge of the defeated nationalist Chinese forces who had fled from the mainland.

Response to the Security Council's call to arms was less than universal. In addition to the United States and South Korea, fifteen other nations— from Australia to Great Britain—participated in the fighting. Overall troop contributions for the period of the war were: Republic of Korea, 500,000; America, 300,000; other, 40,000. Of the 411,000 killed, wounded, captured or missing in action, South Korea suffered 63 percent of the losses; the United States, 33 percent; and the others, 4 percent. Such was the superiority of the North Koreans in equipment and preparations that they were able to push back the South Koreans and the first U.N. troops to the extreme southeast corner of he Korean peninsula, an area that fortunately included the important port of Pusan.

The tide of war turned abruptly on September 15, when General MacArthur undertook a risky maneuver by landing U.N. forces far behind

North Korean lines at Inchon. Large elements of the North Korean army were either destroyed or captured, with the remainder driven beyond the 38th parallel. Supported by the authority of a U.N. General Assembly resolution reiterating the objective of a "unified, independent and democratic Korea," United Nation's forces crossed the 38th parallel on October 7 (Korean time), twelve hours before the U.N. resolution was passed, and pressed forward to the Yalu River, Korea's northern border. Truman backed the decision to cross the parallel—sheer folly in retrospect—because he calculated that a reunified Korea would not only inflict a momentous defeat on the strategy of Soviet world revolution, but also guarantee for Koreans the right of national self-determination. Communist China, inaccurately viewed in Washington as a mere puppet of the Kremlin, had other plans; it felt called upon to prevent the extinction of North Korea. After a skillful buildup whose significance eluded the American command, Chinese armies launched a massive attack in late November. Within a few weeks Peking had hurled the U.N. armies back below the 38th parallel and recaptured the South Korean capitol of Seoul. By early 1959, however, the line had been stabilized, and the U.N. forces counterattacked, pushing the Chinese and North Koreans again beyond the parallel.

On April 11, 1951, President Truman relieved General MacArthur of his dual position as commander of U.N. forces in Korea and of the occupation forces of the United States in Japan. Increasing friction between MacArthur and Truman had resulted from the general's impatience at the restraints placed upon his military activities and his irritating habit of publicly voicing his disagreements with administration and U.N. policy. In particular, MacArthur had complained about the prohibition against bombing enemy sources of supply and communications in what he termed the "privileged sanctuary of Manchuria."

MacArthur's recall set off a violent political debate in the United States—a debate that continued in muted tones until well after the Korean War. The issue for many was whether to limit the war to Korea or to go all out for victory against Peking at the risk of provoking the Soviet Union. For his part, President Truman gave Europe first place and deferred to the opinion of allies in the U.N., in sharp contrast to MacArthur and his supporters, who believed Asia to be the decisive theater in the struggle with communism, and who would have had the United States "go it alone if necessary." A long investigation by two Senate committees ended inconclusively, and the administration adhered to its policy of limited war.

On June 23, 1951, in New York, the head of the Soviet delegation to the United Nations, Yakov A. Malik, responded to a secret inquiry from Washington by stating publicly that the Korean conflict could be settled if both parties so desired. The Soviet delegate's statement led to the opening of armistice negotiations on July 10 at Kaesong, just north of the 38th parallel. There, and later at Panmunjom, the negotiations proceeded with a number of interruptions until July 27, 1953. The questions that proved the most troublesome were the location of the cease-fire line, machinery for enforcing the armistice terms, and repatriation of prisoners. By the spring of 1952, agreement had been reached on all but the last point. The People's Republic of China (Communist China) demanded that all prisoners of war be repatriated, but the U.N. would not agree to compulsory repatriation of thousands of Chinese and North Korean prisoners who were simply unwilling to return to communism. On this issue the negotiations stuck until after the 1952 presidential election.

The Cold War Debate

The repercussions of the Korean War on America were profound. Defense expenditure increased rapidly from $22.3 billion in fiscal year 1951 to $50.4 billion in fiscal year 1953; put differently, defense spending absorbed 5.2 percent of the nation's gross national product in 1950 and 13.5 percent of a much-expanded national product in 1953. As a consequence, the economy experienced an inflationary surge, forcing the president to reimpose direct controls in early 1951. In the spirit of the declared national emergency facing the country, Truman ordered the seizure of the nation's steel mills on April 8, 1952. To avert a strike of their 600,000 workers, the operation of steel mills was turned over to Secretary of Commerce Charles Sawyer in the name of the public interest. Shortly afterward, in *Youngstown Sheet and Tube* v. *Sawyer,* the Supreme Court took a dim view of the administration's conception of presidential prerogative, the majority arguing the invalidity of Truman's action on the grounds that the president's power "must stem either from an act of Congress or from the Constitution itself." The president returned the mills to their owners, with the ensuing strike settled by wage and price increases in July.

In terms of superpower rivalry, the seedtime of the Cold War was over, while prospects of a "hot war" were increasing. In this sense, and in a manner that should not be underestimated, the outspoken, mutual, and unrelieved hostility of the USSR toward the West coincided with what W.W. Rostow once referred to as "the American diplomatic revolution." The communist purges in Czechoslovakia, the Berlin blockade, the triumph of

Mao in China, and the North Korean invasion of South Korea all confirmed basic American policy formulated in the period from 1945 to 1950. In the words of historian Ernest R. May, "Truman and his associates did not just become antipathetic towards the Soviet Union; they adopted the position that communist Russia represented a threat which the United States had to resist, if necessary by war." On the other side, to complete the image of the Cold War emerging in Moscow, Soviet policy makers saw the American decision over Berlin, the creation of the North Atlantic Treaty Organization, and President Truman's swiftness in committing troops to Korea as confirmation of what they came to regard as a threat to their own Eastern European and Far Eastern empire. The Cold War was now fully engaged.

Who was to blame? And which side contributed most to the way in which the Cold War developed? Such questions and attempts to answer them have informed much of the Cold War literature during the past forty years. Realists, who deplored what diplomat George Kennan called the "moralistic-legalistic" approach of the United States to international affairs, argued that had Washington conceded to the Soviets their own sphere of influence and recognized American limitations in controlling events outside the American sphere of influence, the worst episodes of the Cold War could have been avoided. More idealistic commentators in turn condemned the realists for presumably betraying the nation's traditional commitment to the equality of all states, as well as adherence to the right of national self-determination. Moderate revisionists attempted to place the postwar struggle between the two superpowers within the concept of what English historian Herbert Butterfield called the "terrible human predicament," a situation in which even intelligent and reasonably well-intentioned policy makers move inexorably toward conflict and hostility—a situation best captured by Louis J. Halle's image of a scorpion and tarantula in a battle, each impelled to fight the other to the death. Whatever their differences, Realists and their early critics agreed that Soviet aggressiveness was powered by fear and insecurity, the time-honored goals of tsarist expansionism and by the Soviet system itself. All agreed that Moscow generally had only itself to blame for the intensity and duration of the struggle.

The New Left diplomatic historiography that first emerged in the 1960s and 1970s nearly reversed that picture, portraying the Soviets on the defensive and American "aggression" as responsible for the near-catastrophe and bitterness that marked the postwar era. Driven by the structural dynamics of America's inherently expansionist political economy and by an American idealism that casually transformed itself into a kind of missionary anticommunism, the United States after World War II, according to the New Left model, sought to create a freely trading open-door world conducive to providing markets for American surpluses on the one hand and importing vitally needed raw materials on the other. From such a world American policy makers believed democratic institutions and practices would flow, absorbing at once United States interests and ideals. The pursuit of such a world, however, ran counter to Soviet needs and desires, particularly their drive for security against a potential third German invasion in this century. Never ceasing to give Soviet motives and intentions the benefit of the doubt, the New Left's data often produced strained and strange historical explanations with little general appeal outside the profession of history. And even for historians, persuasive arguments have called into question both the New Left's methodology and its integrity.

From another level it is impossible to comprehend the depth of the West's "brave and essential response to Soviet aggression" without first understanding its perception of an ever-shrinking world in which the issues of war and peace were seen as indivisible. Modern warfare, with its awful weapons of destruction and the equally awful contemplation that they could be delivered anywhere in short order—whether by bomber or missile—caused the American people in particular to rethink past policies and their role in the world. Guilt for not having played a part in the League of Nations and felt responsibility for their future and the future of their children prompted Americans to place their faith initially in collective security and the United Nations. The hard fact that the U.N. would or could not play its promised role required a hard decision: Was the United States willing to be the world's policeman? The answer was, of course, yes.

The second part of the problem was to understand the perceived enemy, the Soviet Union. American policy makers were puzzled about the Soviet Union in 1945, in much the same way as they were puzzled about the Soviets in 1917 and remain puzzled today. Washington's attitude toward the Kremlin revolved around a single question: Was Soviet Russia an ideology in the service of a nation-state or a nation-state in the service of an ideology?

Uncertain, fearful perhaps, and with the Nazi experience still in their minds, Americans chose to believe the worst. Historical studies that contend it could have been otherwise miss America's deep, spiritual revulsion toward Bolshevism and fail to place proper emphasis on it. For if it is assumed that policy makers of the West were moved by frightful images, then it must be impossible to expect the leading members of the Truman administration to have behaved differently—to have crawled out of their skins and been transformed. President Truman himself, typical of his countrymen, had no doubt the Kremlin leadership had brought the Cold War upon itself.

Suggested Readings

Donovan, Robert J. *Conflict and Crisis: The Presidency of Harry S. Truman, 1945–1948*. 1977.

———. *The Presidency of Harry S. Truman, 1945–1953*. 1982.

Gaddis, John Lewis. *The United States and the Origins of the Cold War, 1941–1947*. 1972.

———. *Strategies of Containment*. 1982.

Hamby, Alonzo M. *Beyond the New Deal: Harry S. Truman and American Liberalism*. 1973.

Harper, Alan D. *The Politics of Loyalty: The White House and the Communist League, 1946–1952*. 1969.

Hartmann, Susan M. *Truman and the 80th Congress*. 1971.

McCoy, Donald R. and Tuetten, Richard T. *Quest and Response: Minority Rights and the Truman Administration*. 1973.

Markowitz, Norman D. *The Rise and Fall of the People's Century: Henry A. Wallace and American Liberalism, 1941–1948*. 1973.

Martel, Leon. *Lend-Lease, Loans, and the Coming of the Cold War*. 1979.

May, Ernest R. *"Lessons" of the Past*. 1973.

Patterson, James T. *Mr. Republican: A Biography of Robert A. Taft*. 1972.

Phillips, Cabell. *The Truman Presidency*. 1966.

Rees, David. *Korea: The Limited War*. 1964.

Rovere, Richard H. *Senator Joseph McCarthy*. 1959.

Sherwin, Martin J. *A World Destroyed*. 1975.

Siracusa, Joseph M. *The American Diplomatic Revolution: A Documentary History of the Cold War, 1941-1947*. 1976.

———. *New Left Diplomatic Histories and Historians: The American Revisionists*. 1973.

———. *Rearming for the Cold War*. 1983.

Sulzberger, C. L. *Such a Peace: Yalta Revisited*. 1982.

Theoharis, Athan G. *The Yalta Myths*. 1971.

———. *Seeds of Repression*. 1971.

Truman, Harry S. *Memoirs* (2 vols.). 1955.

Weinstein, Allen. *Perjury: The Hiss-Chambers Conflict*. 1978.

Yarnell, Allen. *Democrats and Progressives*. 1974.

Yergin, Daniel. *Shattered Peace*. 1977.

2

General in the White House: The Eisenhower Years

Played out against a backdrop of rising inflation, stalemated armistice talks in Korea, and revelations of graft and corruption in high places, the presidential campaign of 1952 proved long and bitter. There were also some political surprises. In March Harry Truman announced that he would not be a candidate for nomination by the Democratic Convention. Ostensibly concerned with restoring the two-term tradition, Truman conceded that eight years as president had been, "enough and sometimes too much for any man to serve in that capacity"—an opinion incidentally shared by much of the public and most of his critics. This, together with the shocking loss of the New Hampshire Democratic primary contest to Senator Estes Kefauver of Tennessee, who had gained national attention as the chairman of the special Senate Subcommittee to Investigate Interstate Crime, probably persuaded Truman to return to his beloved Independence. In any case, the Republicans could feel fairly confident of regaining the White House, as well as the House and the Senate, particularly if their success in the 1950 midterm elections could serve as a guide. All that remained was to agree on a candidate.

The Republican National Convention met at Chicago in the second week of July. The convention was divided between the supporters of Senator Robert A. Taft of Ohio and the supporters of General Dwight ("Ike") D. Eisenhower. Lawyer, politician, and the son of former President William Howard Taft, Senator Taft rose to prominence as a consistent critic of the New Deal and Fair Deal policies, succeeding the late Senator Arthur Vandenberg as the GOP's chief spokesman in the Senate. Unlike Vandenberg, however, who supported the Truman administration's bipartisan foreign policy in the immediate postwar period, Taft opposed American commitments to Europe as unrealistic, disapproved of the White House's handling of the Korean War, and generally gave credence to the extremist charges of Senator Joseph McCarthy of Wisconsin. All of these and other views strongly endeared Taft to the conservative wing of the party, particularly among those located in the Midwest.

The liberal-internationalist wing of the party, located in the East and the far West, looked to another kind of man as the candidate most likely to return the presidency to the heirs of Herbert Hoover. In turning to General Eisenhower, these Republicans chose a man who had not run for nor held any public office and had, in fact, not voted until 1948, when he was fifty-eight years old. His entire adult life had been spent in the United States Army, principally as an executive and staff officer until his appointment as supreme commander of the Allied Expeditionary Force in World War II. He was subsequently appointed army chief of staff, president of Columbia University, and the first supreme commander of NATO armies. For these accomplishments alone Eisenhower had already become one of the most admired men of his generation. After a series of convention maneuvers, Eisenhower secured victory over Taft on the first ballot. The vice-presidential nomination went to Richard ("Dick") Nixon from California, a rising star in the GOP, an aggressive anticommunist who as a member of the House Un-American Activities Committee achieved national recognition for leading the investigation of State Department official Alger Hiss. In addition to attacking the administration's policies on China and Korea, the Republican platform supported a balanced Federal budget, reduced national debt, and progressive tax relief. The platform also advocated the retention of the Taft-Hartley Act.

Truman's personal choice to succeed to the presidency and continue the Fair Deal was Adlai Stevenson, the popular reform governor of Illinois, elected in 1948 by an unprecedented half-million vote plurality. Lawyer and New Dealer, Stevenson seemed ideally suited to the task. After the necessary prodding, Stevenson traveled from Springfield to Chicago in the third week of July to challenge the Kefauver delegates at the Democratic National Convention; after trailing Kefauver on the first two ballots, Stevenson was elected on the third. Senator John Sparkman of Alabama, a civil rights moderate, was nominated for vice-president. The Democratic platform advocated, among other things, the continuation of the domestic and foreign policy of Franklin Roosevelt and Harry

Truman, as well as the repeal of the Taft-Hartley Act and Federal legislation to secure civil rights.

During the course of the next several months, both standard-bearers campaigned long and hard, Stevenson covering a total of 32,500 miles and making over 200 speeches while Eisenhower covered 33,000 miles and made 270 speeches. Republican party orators charged that the Democratic party was spending the country into bankruptcy, was riddled with graft and corruption, had let too many communists into important posts in Washington, had been in office too long, and had once again been the party of war. Democratic orators replied in kind, charging that the GOP would neither help farmers nor unions, was the party of the rich and the privileged, was without a plan for the defense of Europe against Soviet adventurism, was the party of yesterday, and was likely to bring another depression with bread lines and millions of unemployed. The campaign was especially bitter, and Eisenhower, whose differences with Senator Taft were glossed over, soon shed his image of the proverbial nice guy. Inveighing against "the wasters, the bunglers, the incompetents" and the whole "top to bottom mess" in Washington, Eisenhower not only cast aspersions on Truman's integrity but virtually accused the administration of inviting the communist attack in Korea through inept diplomacy.

The Democrats were vulnerable on two counts. First, they had been in power a long time, since 1932; and, second, the Korean War and the rapid rise of Soviet military power symbolized by the acquisition of the atomic bomb—one of the great espionage coups in modern times—placed the Democrats on the defensive. The Republican strategy was summed up in the simple formula: $K_1 C_2$ = Korea, Crime, Corruption. Urbane, wealthy and sophisticated, Governor Stevenson attracted a wide following in liberal and academic circles, causing yet another kind of problem in a nation traditionally suspicious of intellectuals. Stewart Alsop, a well-known Republican newspaper columnist, went so far as to coin the term *egghead* to describe Stevenson's appeal to intellectuals. Though Stevenson tried to laugh it off— "Eggheads of the world unite, you have nothing to lose but your yoke"—he was hurt by the imagery. Comparisons with the liberator of Western Europe were inevitable if not very productive, leading to a number of campaign ditties that percolated down to the school yard:

> Whistle while you work,
> Stevenson's a jerk,
> Eisenhower's got the power,
> Let him do the work.

Throughout, Stevenson suggested talking "sense to the American people. Let's tell them the truth." But, discussions of "a long, costly, patient struggle against the great enemies of men—war, poverty and tyranny"—were not messages likely to appeal to an electorate surfeited with depression, war, and the threat of war.

As the campaign moved into autumn, GOP fortunes took an unexpected and dangerous turn. The *New York Post* released a story under the headline, "Secret Nixon Fund!" alleging that Ike's running mate enjoyed a high lifestyle paid for out of a secret "millionaire's club" account established for the vice-presidential candidate. Republican strategists panicked as Eisenhower himself prepared to demand Nixon's resignation. With little room to maneuver, the Republican National Committee sent word to Nixon that it had managed to purchase a half-hour of television time; the cost was $75,000 for prime viewing time after the popular "Milton Berle Show." In the so-called Checkers speech of September 23, 1952, which critics contended was pure hokum, Nixon ably defended himself.

The speech began simply enough, seeking to demonstrate that this was not a man with a million dollars in the bank. According to Nixon, he owned a 1950 Oldsmobile, some life insurance, and was buying two houses, one in California and one in Washington, for both of which he owed $30,000. The touch of genius, the final touch which would make the speech a landmark in the brief history of television, came as Nixon concluded:

I should say this—that Pat doesn't have a mink coat. But she does have a respectable cloth coat. And I always tell her that she looks good in anything.

One other thing I should probably tell you, because if I don't they'll be saying this about me, too. We did get something, a gift, after the nomination. A man down in Texas heard Pat on the radio mention the fact that our two youngsters would like to have a dog and, believe it or not, the day before we left on this campaign trip we got a message from Union Station in Baltimore, saying they had a package for us. We went down to get it. You know what it was?

It was a little cocker spaniel dog in a crate that he had sent all the way from Texas—black and white, spotted, and our little girl, Tricia, the six-year-old, named it Checkers. And you know, the kids, like all kids, love that dog, and I just want to say this, right now, that regardless of what they say about it, we're going to keep it.

The impact of the speech was stunning, as sixty million Americans had watched and seen the vice-presidential candidate choking back the tears in close-ups. Before the night was over, the Republican headquarters had received 1,000,000 telegrams in support of Nixon, as well as $60,000 in contributions. This, together with General Eisenhower's late campaign promise to travel to Korea and review the nation's policy there if he were elected, set the stage for what was to be the heaviest election turnout in American history.

Eisenhower won in an electoral vote landslide with an impressive popular majority as nearly 62 million Americans went to the polls. With 33.9 million votes (55.2 percent) to 27.3 million (44.5 percent), Eisenhower outscored Stevenson in the electoral vote category 442 to 89, smashing the traditionally Democratic South. Interestingly, both presidential candidates received the highest popular vote for a winner and loser respectively in the nation's history. At the legislative level, and despite the obvious popularity of General Eisenhower, the Republicans barely managed to capture the House and the Senate. The significance of the election defied simple analysis, for it soon became clear that it was the man and not necessarily the party for which the people had voted. What President Eisenhower would do with this overwhelming "mandate for change" remained to be seen. In any case, Americans looked forward to the first GOP inauguration since 1929, wondering what life would be like under Ike.

The Eisenhower White House

In his inaugural address of January 20, 1953, President Eisenhower uniquely captured the mood of the American people. "We sense with all our faculties," observed Eisenhower, "that forces of good and evil are massed and armed and opposed as rarely before in history." In the face of a tumultuous half-century of change and violence, the president exhorted his fellow citizens to summon their collective wit and will to meet the question of the age: "How far have we come in man's long pilgrimage from darkness toward the light. Are we nearing the light—a day of freedom and of peace for all mankind? Or are the shadows of another night closing in upon us?" Having said that, Eisenhower then set out the rules of conduct by which the United States would be known to all peoples. Among these were: "We hold it to be the first task of statesmanship to develop the strength that will deter the forces of aggression and promote the conditions of peace"; "we stand ready to engage with any and all others in joint effort to remove the causes of mutual fear and distrust among nations, so as to make possible drastic reduction of armaments"; "we shall never try to placate an aggressor by the false and wicked bargaining of trading honor for security"; and, finally, "we shall strive to help" proven friends of freedom "to achieve their own security and well-being," though "we shall count upon them to assume, within the limits of their resources, their full and just burdens in the common defense of freedom." While his words faithfully echoed the sentiments of the strictures found in the New Testament, the president, once in power, surrounded himself with the best minds to be found in the boardrooms of the nations's leading corporations.

In what was clearly meant to be seen as a businessmen's administration, Ike appointed, among others, the president of General Motors, Charles E. Wilson, as his secretary of defense; the president of (Mark Hanna's former firm) M.A. Hanna and Co., George Humphrey, as secretary of the treasury; and one of the country's highest-paid corporate lawyers, John Foster Dulles, as secretary of state. Dulles, who was shortly to become one of the most influential men to hold that office in modern times, was also one of the most experienced in the ways of diplomacy, with service dating back to the Paris Peace Conference of 1919. Dulles gave Eisenhower the impression, in the president's words, that he "seems to sense the intricacies of what those people are driving at better than anyone I have listened to." Unfortunately for some, Dulles's apparent highmindedness and moralistic rigidity made the otherwise logical appointment a difficult pill to swallow.

Others in the cabinet included several automobile distributors, a manufacturer from New England, a conservation specialist in agriculture, and the wife of a prominent Texas publisher. The one exception in the cabinet was the secretary of labor, Martin Durkin, who was both a Democrat and president of a plumbers' union, prompting the *New Republic* to proclaim the cabinet "eight millionaires and a plumber." The administration's principal theme at home was, in the words of the secretary of defense, "What was good for our country was good for General Motors and vice versa."

Unlike Truman, whose induction into the presidency brought with it a sense of awe and a public plea for the prayers of his fellow citizens, Eisenhower approached the duties of the Oval Office with a sense of relative equanimity. According to his first diary entry: "My first day at the President's desk. Plenty of worries and difficult problems. But such has been my portion for a long time—the result is that this just seems like a continuation of all I've been doing since July 1941—even before that." Not unlike his predecessor, Eisenhower rapidly identified himself with the national forces of moderation. In 1949 in a speech to the American Bar Association as president of Columbia University, the future chief executive declared: "The path to America's future lies down the middle of the road between the unfettered power of concentrated wealth . . . and the unbridled power of statism or partisan interests." During the course of his presidency, Eisenhower seldom if ever deviated from his moderate principles, his middle-of-the-road position, on most questions. Perhaps such an approach to politics satisfied neither the liberals nor the conservatives; it did, however, satisfy the majority of Americans who were in no mood to witness the dismantling of major New Deal and Fair Deal legislation, particularly Social Security.

The Korean Settlement

True to his campaign pledge, Eisenhower visited Korea in December 1952, letting it be known that he advocated the United Nations' position on the prisoners of war. He was in fact determined to bring the war to an end, and after his inauguration allowed Secretary of State Dulles to spread the word that unless an armistice were declared soon, Washington might find it necessary "to blast Manchuria north of the Yalu if the stalemate continued." To this covert threat to use atomic weapons against China, and his removal of President Truman's ban on operations from Taiwan (Formosa) against the mainland in early 1953, the president later attributed the decision of Peking to accept U.N. terms. Armistice negotiations were resumed in April after a suspension of six months. For reasons of their own, the communists were now prepared to make concessions on the thorny issue of the prisoners of war, and, in spite of the violent opposition of South Korean President Syngman Rhee, an armistice agreement was signed at Panmunjom on July 27, 1953.

Meeting in Berlin in early 1954, the Big Four foreign ministers agreed that a conference on the Korean question, among other things, should be held in Geneva in April. There, South Korea and fifteen of the United Nations that had participated in the police action confronted North Korea and her allies China and the Soviet Union. A U.N. proposal for the unification of the Korean peninsula after supervised free elections could be held throughout the country was rejected by the North Koreans, and no agreement was reached.

In the absence of a settlement or even the prospect of one, the armistice continued to prevail. A treaty of mutual defense, similar to others then being negotiated by Washington in the Pacific region, had been signed by representatives of the United States and the Republic of Korea a year earlier, with South Korea consenting to the stationing of American armed forces "in and about" its territory. Two American army divisions remained in Korea technically under the auspices of the United Nations.

The New Look

President Eisenhower entered office committed at once to taking a "New Look" at national security and to pursuing a policy of fiscal restraint; in effect, he sought to cut the size of the armed forces without jeopardizing America's defense commitments. By October 1953 a new planning document (National Security Policy Planning Paper Number 162/2) had been approved by the president, and three months later Secretary of State Dulles publicly unveiled the new policy of "massive retaliation." The United States, Dulles explained, had decided "to depend primarily upon a great capacity to retaliate, instantly, by means and at places of our own choosing." Accordingly, the United States would no longer constrain itself to meet communist military probes with a conventional weapons response as it had in Korea. In future, he proposed "more basic security at less cost"—or "more bang for the buck," to use Secretary of Defense Charles Wilson's phrase.

The doctrine of massive retaliation provided the guiding principle of American nuclear strategy for the remainder of the 1950s and ensured a structure of limited conventional, but substantial nuclear, forces. The doctrine reigned supreme in a decade of international troubles despite the fact that in the crises the Eisenhower administration faced, it never retaliated massively, it seldom employed threats of massive retaliation, and it never really utilized the strategic forces it had acquired.

The intellectual, no less than the moral, validity of the concept of massive retaliation was increasingly questioned and challenged during the mid- and late-1950s, particularly in regard to the buildup of Soviet nuclear weapons and delivery capacity. In 1953, less than a year after the United States had done so, the Soviet Union exploded its own hydrogen bomb and then proceeded to to develop bombers that could reach targets in Europe and on the American mainland. But, the long, intercontinental flight distances to American targets and the need to overfly Canada, where warning and intercept installations could be based, lessening the probable penetration capabilities of Soviet strategic bombers, led Moscow, in turn, to examine alternatives and ultimately to emphasize strategic missile development. The redirection of Soviet resources soon bore fruit.

On August 3, 1957, a Soviet surface-to-surface (SS-6) intercontinental ballistic missile (ICBM) rocketed several thousand miles from its launch pad to impact on Russian Siberia; within two months, on October 4, 1957, this same type of rocket successfully launched a man-made earth satellite into space. The satellite, Sputnik I, an artificial moon with a diameter of 22 inches and a weight of 184 pounds—eight times heavier than that contemplated by American scientists—moved in a maximum orbit of 560 miles above the earth at a speed of 18,000 miles an hour. A month later the Soviets launched a second satellite, weighing more than one thousand pounds.

The effect on American thinking was both dramatic and humbling, particularly as it struck a blow at the presumed superiority of American technology. Eisenhower's response was twofold: the acceleration of the United States' own earth satellite program, which resulted in the launching of Explorer I in January 1958; and the adoption of an $877 million education aid bill, the National Defense Education Act, in September 1958, aimed at strengthening the American education system so that it would meet the broad and increasing demands imposed upon it by consideration of basic national security. The NDEA, designed as an emergency undertaking to be terminated after four years, provided loans, fellowships to future college teachers, and grants to states to help locate and guide able students, as well as to provide equipment for teaching science, mathematics, and modern foreign languages.

The ushering in of the missile age had other, more serious implications. The addition of ICBMs to the Soviet strategic arsenal not only exposed the United States directly to massive nuclear attack for the first time, but also substantially increased the vulnerability of American strategic forces to a surprise attack, fulfilling the technical requirements of the presumption of a Soviet first-strike mentality envisaged by NSC 68 in 1950. Clearly, nuclear vulnerability undermined the fundamental basis of the doctrine of massive retaliation. Despite charges, first, of a "bomber gap" and then of a "missile gap," the Eisenhower administration proceeded cautiously with the continued development and deployment of countermeasures such as the Thor intermediate range ballistic missile (IRBM), the Atlas and Titan ICBMs, and with the Polaris submarine-launched ballistic missile (SLBM) programs. The general-turned-politician rested secure in knowledge gleaned from U-2 reconnaissance flights over the USSR that the Soviets had not in fact built a nuclear strike force capable of crippling America's deterrence.

What also changed in the Eisenhower years was the American attitude toward nuclear arms agreements. The formula of general disarmament, which persisted despite the demise of the Baruch Plan, was gradually supplanted by the concept of partial arms limitations. This concept was mainly aimed at the stabilization and control of the central nuclear balance— the management of arms competition—rather than its elimination. Such an approach underlay the president's "Open Skies" proposal of 1955 insofar as the unimpeded disclosure of information originating from aerial surveillance was thought to be the critical safeguard against the prospect of a surprise attack. Obsessive of its secrets, including Soviet inferiority in duplicating American miniaturization of their H-bomb, the Kremlin rejected the proposal outright; and although the two superpowers held intermittent discussions on the subject over the remainder of the 1950s, they singularly failed to reach agreement, the all-important question of verification continuing to be the perennial stumbling block. The arms control approach as opposed to general disarmament extended beyond Eisenhower, however, and would prevail in time to achieve tangible though limited results.

McCarthy's Last Stand

With the Republicans in control of the White House, Wisconsin Senator Joseph R. McCarthy, perhaps the most formidable and gifted American demagogue of the century, proceeded to step up his crusade to purify the American body politic of any and all traces of communism, real or otherwise. Though few would care to admit it, McCarthy had behind him at the height of his power many of the nation's most respected politicians, Republicans as well as some conservative Democrats; the powerful Hearst newspaper network was also solidly for him. More significantly, according to a Gallup poll of January 15, 1954, 50 percent of the American people had a "favorable opinion" of the Senator. At the root of McCarthyism lay American disillusionment with the aftermath of World War II, particularly growing evidence of Soviet betrayal of the lofty aims of the war in eastern Europe and, on a more sinister level, the discovery of evidence of Soviet espionage in the United States. Sociologists and some political commentators have been concerned to relate the McCarthy phenomenon to a broader stream of political and social protest in America, especially that of victims of the so-called status revolution used to explain the growth of protest movements in the late nineteenth century.

Whatever the origin of McCarthyism, President Eisenhower showed little inclination to confront the senator publicly, though it is equally clear the president harbored a strong dislike for the man and his methods. In the opening months of the administration, McCarthy attacked the presumably subversive elements in the Voice of America and the Overseas Book Programs, demanding the removal of works even remotely associated with communists. Without mentioning McCarthy by name, Eisenhower warned against joining the book burners.

McCarthy also sought unsuccessfully to stop the nomination of Charles

E. Bohlen as ambassador to the Soviet Union on the grounds of his close connections with the foreign policies of Franklin Roosevelt and Harry Truman. As chairman of the Senate Permanent Investigating Subcommittee of the Government Operations Committee, McCarthy then conducted a series of hearings, lasting to 1954, on the role of presumed communist influence in government and in other areas. Congressional committees simultaneously investigated communism in the fields of education and entertainment. Again, careers in and out of Washington were ruined through the device of accusation and guilt by association.

In early 1954 the administration finally found itself forced to take a tougher public position against McCarthy. When the army failed to take punitive action against a Major Irving Peress, a dentist accused of communist activities (Peress was granted an honorable discharge), McCarthy inveighed against the major's commandant, General Ralph Zwicker, as a coddler of communists and demanded that Zwicker be relieved of his command. After some hesitation in the direction of placating the Senator, Secretary of the Army Robert Stevens remonstrated that he would "never accede to the abuse of Army personnel . . . never accede to their browbeating and humiliation." The stage was now set for the final act in the senator's crusade against communism.

After an investigation of communist subversion at Fort Monmouth, New Jersey, in late 1953 and early 1954, the Senate Permanent Subcommittee on Investigations, with the senator from Wisconsin in the role of a witness, convened in April to examine allegations made by the secretary of the army that McCarthy and the subcommittee's counsel, Roy M. Cohn, sought by improper means to obtain preferential treatment for a committee consultant, Private G. David Schine. The subcommittee also agreed to look into McCarthy's countercharges that Secretary of the Army Stevens and several of his associates had engaged in a campaign to discourage further investigation of alleged communist subversion at Fort Monmouth. The proceedings were televised over a period of thirty-five days lasting from April 22 to June 17; the featured speakers in what soon became called the Army-McCarthy hearings featured the senator and special army counsel Joseph N. Welch.

In a nation increasingly addicted to television viewing, the Army-McCarthy hearings became compelling drama, the audience at times reaching twenty million people. After thirty-five days of public exposure, the American people had seen and heard enough to be persuaded that McCarthy, sinister looking with his black, bushy eyebrows and five o'clock shadow, had indeed used improper means in trying to get preferred treatment for Private Schine, despite the subcommittee's majority report exonerating the senator from charges of improper influence.

McCarthy's popularity among the American public plunged from 50 percent to 34 percent, according to a June 1954 Gallup poll. Some, including Republican committee member Senator Charles E. Potter of Michigan, were convinced that the principal accusation of each side was borne out and that perjury had indeed been committed. In August the Senate established a select committee to investigate McCarthy's own activities in the Senate. On December 2, 1954, McCarthy became only the fourth member in the history of the United States to be censured, with a final vote of 67–22. The resolution of condemnation—the word censure was not employed—found that McCarthy's actions were "contrary to Senatorial ethics and tend to bring the Senate into dishonor and disrepute, to obstruct the constitutional processes of the Senate, and to impair its dignity. "His own reputation in tatters, McCarthy's influence rapidly declined until the time of his death in May 1957.

The war of words against McCarthy should in no way be construed as a lesser desire on the part of the Eisenhower administration to deal harshly with the perpetrators of the communist conspiracy at home. Within his first two years in office, Eisenhower signed into law numerous pieces of antisubversive legislation. Various provisions of this body of legislation imposed legal, political, and economic penalties on Communist party members, and took away the rights, privileges, and immunities that otherwise legal bodies ordinarily have under the Federal government; granted immunity from prosecution to certain suspected persons in order to obtain the conviction of communists; provided for the loss of citizenship by those advocating the overthrow of the government by force and violence; and increased penalties for those harboring or concealing communists who were fugitives from justice. As a result of administration enforcement of antisubversive laws, boasted the president in August 1954, "forty-one top communist leaders have been convicted, thirty-five more are indicted and scheduled for trial, and 105 subversive aliens have been deported." A year earlier, in June, the president adamantly refused to save atomic-secret spies Julius and Ethel Rosenberg from death in the electric chair. "The execution of two human beings is a grave matter," remarked the chief executive shortly before their deaths and in his second refusal of executive clemency. "But even graver is the thought of the millions of dead whose deaths may be directly attributable to what these spies have done." Two very probable spies went to their deaths without flinching or showing remorse.

The Fifties

The Eisenhower years, now looked upon with a good deal of nostalgic fondness as "Happy Days," were an era of stunning prosperity especially for the upper 20 percent of a population that grew by more than twenty-eight million souls in the 1950s. Millions of Americans, continuing the traditional westward movement, migrated to California and the Southwest. By the early 1960s, California had surpassed New York as the most populous state in the Union, with all the attendant political clout. Other immigrants doubled the population of Florida, thanks largely to the widespread production of the air conditioner. Even the recessions of late 1953 and 1957 proved manageable, mainly through the exercise of the administration's strict monetarist policies and fiscal restrain, i.e., controlling the money supply and holding down Federal appropriations. Americans on the whole were eminently content with their own way of life, perceived as an ideal blend of private initiative and government regulation, with provision for a limited program of social welfare. Not only were people becoming prosperous, but the fruits of wartime technology were now reaped by the general public in the form of super cars, super highways, and inexpensive housing, mainly in the surburbs—the faceless dormitories of the middle class who commuted to the city to work.

The administration played its own role in determining these developments. The Housing Act of 1954 provided for the construction of thirty-five thousand units in one year, allowing preferential refuge for those displaced by slum clearance and other public improvements. Subsequent housing acts raised maximum permissible mortgage amounts, but required cash payments, and generally liberalized the terms of down payment. For the man on the land, Eisenhower sought to construct a farm program aimed at bringing food and fiber supplies into line with demand without undercutting Federal price supports; accordingly, Secretary of Agriculture Ezra Taft Benson turned to the establishment of a sliding scale of price supports to curb unbalanced farm production flowing from the price-depressing effect of $2.5 billion worth of farm products housed in Federal storage.

Though Congress had already made a high-speed Federal highway system eligible for Federal funds in 1944, it was not until 1956 that much was done about it. At President Eisenhower's urging, the Federal Highway Act was enacted. Essentially, it provided for the spending of $32 billion over a thirteen-year period for the construction of a forty-one thousand mile interstate highway system (1,944 more miles were authorized later) and for completing construction of the Federal aid system of highways, the government contributing 90 percent to the former and 50 percent to the latter to be financed by new taxes on gasoline and other highway-user items. Since then nearly $175 billion has been spent, and an average of forty-five thousand people have been working full time; during the decade of the sixties, the system grew forty miles a week. More than fifteen hundred miles of the interstate highways in forty-six states remain unfinished. Still, it is possible to drive from coast to coast wihout a stoplight.

In other domestic landmarks the administration established the Department of Health, Education and Welfare, with Mrs. Oveta Culp Hobby as the first secretary in 1953; authorized the establishment of the United States Air Force Academy in Colorado Springs, Colorado, in 1954; and provided funds for the construction of the St. Lawrence Seaway, a 27-foot-deep channel between Montreal and Lake Erie, in the same year. The year 1954 also witnessed the enactment of the Atomic Energy Act, which opened the door to private enterprise in producing and marketing electric power generated from nuclear reactors. The act, which also allowed for the transfer of atomic weapons secrets to America's Western European allies, marked the first major revision of the basic law governing atomic energy since 1946.

Despite the legislative activity and the popularity of the administration, the congressional elections of November 1954 went badly for the GOP, proving once again that the chief asset of the Republican party was the president of the United States. The Democrats overturned the Republican majority in Congress with a margin of twenty-nine in the House and a margin of one in the Senate. And in 1955 even the president seemed in mortal danger from a coronary thrombosis he suffered in September. Though he resumed some duties within a week, it would require months of good care before he was up to full strength. By early 1956, the president felt confident enough physically to declare that he would seek the renomination of his party later in the year.

The Homogenizing of America

In addition to living in houses and driving automobiles that looked alike, Americans in the 1950s were conditioned to think alike, the result of the invasion of the television into the family home. Unlike radio, which also had its place in the family unit, television required little if any energy to watch and no imagination at all. Commercial television itself began in the United States in the late 1940s, though experiments in transmitting picture signals through the air waves had begun in England in the late 1920s. Although it may be difficult for television-addicted Americans to believe today, television was not an overnight success. Until about 1951 or even later, commercial radio competed successfully for big network entertainment. The main problem was that television reception was relatively poor. Large home antennas were required to receive even local stations as viewers complained of the "snowstorm" effect, which often made viewing nearly impossible. But, of course, bad reception or not, people did watch. The television age had been born, and the first television generation was getting its education.

What did Americans watch? For the more discerning, television was, as a Federal Communications Commissioner would later say, a "wasteland," though few would deny the merits of such first-class live drama as the celebrated "Playhouse 90." For the lowbrow, i.e., for most Americans, television fare was entertaining if at times dismal. A few of the top-rated shows of the 1950s included "Sid Caeser," "Milton Berle," "Jack Benny" (all done live), "Ozzie and Harriet," "Our Miss Brooks," and "Dragnet." For the children there was "Howdy Doody," "Pinky Lee," and "Hopalong Cassidy."

The real power of television was not, however, revealed in the programs themselves, most of which proved easily forgettable, but in other areas; namely, the stunning impact of television commercials replete with their "hidden persuaders." Indeed, the ad-man in his grey flannel suit and buttoned-down shirt became a kind of hero of the 1950s, at once a con artist and a brilliant student of his culture. The public was seduced, and they loved it. The television advertisements created minor legends and the best of them passed into Madison Avenue folklore. Americans knew that Viceroy cigarettes were the thinking man's filter, that Geritol cured tired blood, that you could always tell a Halo girl, and that you should see the USA in your Chevrolet.

Even more indicative of the things to come was the revelation of the enormous potential of television to intrude itself into people's lives by bringing them face-to-face with real-life drama. The first such drama focused on the hearings into organized crime conducted by Senator Kefauver who proved to be the star of his own show; his co-star was New York underworld figure Frank Costello. The Costello interviews in March 1951 scored 70 percent in the influential televison ratings, better than the World Series. General MacArthur's tearful farewell to a packed Congress, Nixon's "Checkers" speech, and the Army-McCarthy hearings all involved the casual viewers in a manner previously thought impossible.

The debate about the merits of television has gone on unabated since those early days. Social commentator and writer E. B. White once observed that television could either become a great boon or an inordinate distraction, perhaps the most perfect opiate the world has ever seen. The per capita average of television viewing in the United States rose to 8.5 hours per day in the 1980s. For children it was the veritable invasion of the body snatchers. Between the ages of six and eighteen, the average American child spent approximately fifteen to sixteen thousand hours in front of a television set, in contrast to approximately thirteen thousand hours in school. During this time, the same average child witnessed two hundred thousand acts of violence, including fifty thousand murders and five hundred thousand advertisements. Some critics of the medium argued that television tended to damage a child's critical abilities, others disagreed. What could not be doubted was the extent to which television homogenized Americans themselves—regional dialects, outlooks, even the difference between adulthood and childhood tended to be blurred as all adult secrets came under the scrutiny of youthful observers.

The book that best conceptualized the American way of doing things in the 1950s was William H. Whyte's *The Organization Man,* the perfect complement to the centrifugal forces of the culture makers of the time. *The Organization Man* served both as hero and model of young men everywhere, though to be sure there were rebels without a particular cause opting out of the system albeit in as conspicuous a fashion as possible. Whyte, an editor of *Fortune* magazine, read the times well. The one thing that struck Whyte about the United States economy in the 1950s was the increasing decline of small business; equally significant, the decline was unlamented. Small business had been replaced by big business, but not the big business of the robber barons of an earlier period. Rather, small business was replaced by the gentle, giant Big Brother organization, which really "cared" about society, its environment, and its employees.

Who was the Organization Man? For one thing he was young, in his thirties; for another, he was a veteran of World War II who subsequently obtained a university education courtesy of the G.I. Bill. He was unmistakably dressed in his gray flannel suit, snap brim hat, narrow dark tie, and shirt with a button-down collar—the sort of character often portrayed by actors such as Jack Lemmon in the movie *The Apartment.* An aspiring executive in a large corporation, he was upwardly mobile and determined to be a corporate success; in fact, it was the attraction of working in a large company that appealed to him and was his distinctive characteristic.

The organization—whether a corporate giant, Federal agency, or a great university—became the principal bestower of gratification and success. Whyte observed that with few exceptions all these institutions were as alike as the attitudes and expectations of their executives. The ultimate goal of the Organization Man was to be seen as a good team player, for there was no place for the individual or the genuinely creative genius unless, of course, he was prepared to play on the team. The Organiztion Man was a familiar if indistinguishable face in suburbia, played a community role, bowled on Friday evenings, and attended church (preferably Episcopalian or Presbyterian) regularly. Put another way, he sought to be Everyman. The trick of success, however, was to play Everyman so well that he could eventually reach the top—the reward reserved for one who was most like everyone else. Moreover, the Organization Man was constantly monitored to make certain he continued to be a team player, subjecting himself to a battery of "personality" tests designed to detect deviation from the norm. To round out the family requirement, the Organization Wife was supposed to look like Doris Day, while the children attended an Organization School.

Whyte reproduced the personality test used to screen prospective executives for Sears Roebuck, considered a model corporation of its kind in the 1950s. Typical of the questions asked were: "Who did you love most—your father or your mother?" Or, "Which would you rather do—read a book or go bowling?" Men who chose their father, and preferred bowling to reading were assured every opportunity to succeed.

The ascendance of the Organization Man in his Brooks Brothers suit led many social commentators to celebrate the so-called American consensus, which tended to highlight the values the majority of Americans shared rather than those on which they diverged. Less sanguine critics of consensus tended to perceive a darker, more sinister side. In his study *The Power Elite,* published in 1956, C. Wright Mills found cold comfort in the doctrine of consensus, perceiving in it a new and frightening version of the totalitarian state. As part of a new elite, Mills contended, the *Organization Man* was more interested in furthering his own interests than in the interests of the people as a whole. Whatever position he took on the matter, Whyte's *Organization Man* and Mills's *Power Elite* became classic expressions of the decade.

A Republican Foreign Policy

By 1954 Washington was bearing 70 percent of the cost of French military effort directed against the nationalist insurgency of North Vietnam's communist leader Ho Chi Minh. In spite of such massive material aid and after eight years' effort, the war went badly for the French, reaching crisis proportions in the spring when a combined army of twenty thousand French and loyal Vietnamese found itself surrounded and isolated by a superior force of Viet Minh troops in the frontier fortress of Dienbienphu. In urgent appeals to Washington, Paris warned that without direct American military intervention all was lost, and the way was paved for the communist conquest of Indochina, perhaps all of Southeast Asia. To Eisenhower, who likened the situation to the falling of a row of dominoes, and even more so to Secretary of State Dulles, such a challenge merited a response. Congress, as well as the president, strongly opposed unilateral intervention, however, and the British were reluctant to undermine the forthcoming international conference meeting in Geneva to deal with the problems of Korea and Indochina. Consequently, the French capitulated on May 7.

Having failed to reach agreement on Korea, the Geneva Conference (April 26 to July 21, 1954) turned to Indochina with greater expectations. Dulles took little part in this phase of proceedings. The armistice terms ended the fighting in Indochina and divided Vietnam at the 17th parallel of north latitude. The Viet Minh, officially the Democratic Republic of Vietnam, was to take the north; South Vietnam was to take all lands south of the line. The division was temporary until the country was to be united after general elections scheduled for July 1956. Though the elections never took place, few doubted the likely outcome. "I have never talked or corresponded with a person knowledgeable in Indochinese affairs," recalled President Eisenhower in his memoirs, "who did not agree that had elections been held as of the time of the fighting, possibly 80 percent of the population would have voted for the Communist Ho Chi Minh as their leader."

Since it appeared that only international action would prevent the further advance of communism in the region, Dulles initiated the creation of a Southeast Asia Treaty Organization (SEATO) to serve as a barrier to communist advances in Southeast Asia, as NATO served in Europe. The only Asian nations that could be counted upon were the Philippines, Thailand, and Pakistan. Delegates from these three countries, together with representatives of the United States, Great Britain, France, Australia, and New Zealand, met at Manila in September 1954. The ensuing collective defense treaty followed the pattern of the Australia-New Zealand and Philippines treaties rather than the Three Musketeers' language of the NATO treaty, i.e., a promise to "act to meet the common danger in accordance with its constitutional processes." Among other things it declared through an attached protocol that "the free territory under the jurisdiction of the state of Vietnam" should be eligible for both protective features and economic benefits deriving from the treaty. Within a year the newly proclaimed Republic of Vietnam (South Vietnam), under the leadership of Ngo Dinh Diem, would draw closer to American sponsorship.

In its concern over the threat of communism in Asia and elsewhere, Washington had largely ignored troubling conditions in Latin America, where the need for economic and social reforms was imperative. Before long, dramatic happenings alerted the Eisenhower administration to the urgency of the Latin American situation. The first of these critical events was the adoption of an openly leftist line in both domestic policy and in alignment with the Soviets in the United Nations by President Jacobo Arbenz Guzman (1951–1954) of Guatemala. To Secretary of State Dulles, any leftist beachhead in the Americas, no matter how small, seemed a direct threat to the security of the United States and its sister republics. Accordingly, in June 1954 Guzman was overthrown by a fellow countryman, Colonel Carlos Castillo Armas, who was assisted by American arms and several planes provided by the Central Intelligence Agency.

If the brief apparition of communist power in Guatemala shocked the Eisenhower administration, a ruder shock was the series of violent demonstrations against vice-president Nixon during his tour of South America in the spring of 1958. Nixon departed for South America in April, announcing that the purpose of his journey was to show "that these countries are not only our neighbors but our best friends." The vice-president's reception varied from country to country, but in Lima, Peru, and in Caracas, Venezuela, his life (and that of Mrs. Nixon) was in peril. Though Nixon attributed his problems in part to communist elements, there was also a widespread popular impression that Washington had become too friendly to dictatorships in Latin America; indeed, the United States traditionally made no distinction between dictatorial and democratic regimes in its official relationships.

The year 1956, a presidential election year, witnessed two major foreign policy crises, both of which tested the leadership of the Eisenhower administration to the limit. The first crisis was produced by Soviet suppression of an attempted anticommunist revolution in Hungary; the second crisis was precipitated by an attack on Egypt by Israel, France, and Great Britain.

The death of Josef Stalin in March 1953 was the prelude to the rise of power in the Kremlin of a leader whose aims were identical to Stalin's but whose methods were more flexible, more seductive, and perhaps more dangerous. Stalin's first successor as premier, Georgi M. Malenkov, was promptly sidelined in favor of Nikolai A. Bulganin, while Nikita S. Khrushchev, the crude but brilliant Communist party secretary, emerged as the effective Soviet leader. By 1958 Khrushchev would also assume the duties of premier. In foreign policy, the new regime set out to entice the uncommitted nations instead of frightening them; another important characteristic was a degree of relaxation in Moscow's control of communist parties and governments in the Soviet sphere of Europe.

In Hungary dissatisfaction took a more fundamental turn. Anti-Soviet and antigovernment riots led to the installation, on October 24, 1956, of a new regime headed by Imre Nagy. Several days later the communist Nagy admitted noncommunists to his government. On November 1 Budapest repudiated the Warsaw Alliance, declared Hungary a neutralist state—like its neighbor, Austria, which reemerged as an independent state in 1955—and appealed to the United Nations for assistance. By this time the Soviet leadership, fearful of appearing weak, had had enough. Temporarily withdrawing its tanks and troops from the Hungarian capital, it sent them back in force, quelled the popular uprising in the city, and stage-managed the installation of a new communist regime headed by Janos Kadar, who obediently invited Soviet assistance into Hungary. Nagy, who had been granted a safe conduct by the Kremlin, was executed. A virtually unarmed citizenry proved no match for Soviet tanks.

No aid came from the West, despite Secretary of State Dulles' brave talk of the "liberation" of peoples under the yoke of communism. Within two weeks thousands of Hungarians died fighting, while several hundred thousand fled into exile. Even if the United States, or NATO for that matter, had wished to intervene, it would have been seriously hampered by contemporary events in the Middle East.

The Eisenhower administration pursued its containment policy in the Middle East in three ways: first, by attempting to resolve disputes that otherwise might tempt Soviet interference within the region, particularly the quarrel between Israel and its neighbor, and controversies between Egypt and Iran on the one hand and Great Britain on the other; second, by raising living standards through developmental assistance; and third, by strengthening the area's military potential, as well as its willingness, to resist Soviet-sponsored subversion. This third line of approach received its main impetus from Dulles, whose general policy was to encircle the USSR with military alliances. What NATO did for Europe and SEATO did for Southeast Asia, the Baghdad Pact was supposed to do for the region stretching from Pakistan to Turkey. An alliance of "northern tier" states—Turkey, Pakistan, Iran, Iraq, and Britain—was set in place by early 1955, but with the United States reserving formal membership. Before the ink was dry, Egypt announced a barter deal of cotton for Czech arms, followed by news of an alliance and a joint command between Egypt, Syria, and Saudi Arabia.

Washington and London attempted to recover their forfeited goodwill in Cairo by proposing to aid President Gamal Abdel Nasser in financing a new high dam at Aswan on the Nile. When Nasser's ambassador traveled to Washington in July 1956 to accept the loan, he was told abruptly that the offer had been withdrawn. To Dulles, Nasser had become a poor economic and political risk. Nasser was infuriated while the British were annoyed at not having been consulted on what had been a joint offer. The Egyptian leader responded dramatically on July 26 with the nationalization of the Suez Canal, owned chiefly by British and French stockholders, and the vital link between Western Europe and the Middle Eastern oil fields. The Egyptian government proposed to collect the tolls and apply part of the proceeds to the construction of the Aswan Dam. Negotiations to arbitrate the difference led nowhere and were compounded by the fact that neither London nor Paris had any confidence in Nasser whose pan-Arab nationalism was seen as abetting rebellion against France in Algeria and British influence in Arabia.

Fearful for its very existence, Israel was the first nation to act. On October 29, 1956, less than a week after the start of the Hungarian revolt, Israeli forces struck without warning at Egyptian positions in the Gaza Strip and the Sinai peninsula. The Egyptian armies were overwhelmed, great stores of arms were captured and the invaders pushed on across the Sinai toward the Suez Canal. Officially, and probably in collusion with the Israelis, Britain and France requested Israel and Egypt to accept a cease-fire, and when Cairo predictably refused, announced they would occupy positions along the canal to separate the belligerents and keep the canal open—the pretext for intervention. Their real purpose was to bring Nasser down. On November 5, Anglo-French troops parachuted into the canal area, followed a day later by a naval invasion at Port Said.

Eisenhower reacted angrily to these resorts to force in violation of the United Nations Charter by one friendly state and two important allies; he made it clear to his allies that he was fully committed to support the victims of aggression and that, under the circumstances, he would not be bound by traditional alliances. The president also made it clear that he did not care in the slightest whether he was re-elected or not. On November 5, the General Assembly recommended the creation of an Emergency Force for Palestine, which was plainly perceived as a face-saving mechanism. Under combined international pressure the British, the French, and the Israelis agreed the next day to a cease-fire. London and Paris had suffered a humiliating retreat. Nasser, in spite of a crippling military defeat and loss of territory to the Israelis, had been saved from complete disaster by the intervention of the U.N., backed by the superpowers. Aid for the Aswan Dam was ultimately provided by Moscow.

What did the United States hope to achieve? According to one senior Middle East correspondent, "President Eisenhower's insistence that the rule of law be obeyed was one of the high points of his presidency."

The 1956 Presidential Election

The road to the 1956 presidential election held few surprises. Not unexpectedly, the Republican National Convention renominated Eisenhower and Nixon, though plainly the president was still more popular among the electorate than the party he represented. And again, the Democratic National Convention nominated Stevenson. The vice-presidential nominee, Senator Kefauver of Tennessee, was chosen in an open contest by the delegates themselves after a spirited challenge by young Senator John F. Kennedy of Massachusetts.

The impact of the Hungarian uprising and the Middle East crisis notwithstanding, the most remarkable aspect of the campaign was the absence of an issue. Economically, Americans were better off than they had ever been; inflation, which averaged less than 1.5 percent a year in the Eisenhower years, was hardly a cause of concern. Toward the end of the campaign, Stevenson aroused some interest with proposals to reduce the draft and to suspend hydrogen bomb tests, neither of which seemed persuasive against the criticism of the general in the White House.

The only real difference between the candidates, reported one observer, was that "the incautious Mr. Stevenson is promising the millennium tomorrow; the more cautious President Eisenhower promises it the day after." In any case, President Eisenhower won by a landslide, the most spectacular victory since Franklin Roosevelt's triumph over Alfred M. Landon in 1930: 457 to 73 in electoral votes and 35,590,472 (57.4 percent) to 26,022,752 (42 percent) in popular votes. There were also a number of historic firsts: Eisenhower became the first Republican in the twentieth century to win two successive presidential elections; the first president in the nation's history to be legally debarred from a third term of office; and, more ominously, the first president-elect since 1848 who failed to carry both the Senate and the House. The Democrats won resounding victories in Congress with margins of 234 to 201 in the House and 49 to 47 in the Senate; in the midterm elections of 1958, the opposition would improve these margins to 282 to 154 and 64 to 34, respectively.

Fully conscious of his one-man victory, the president, in his State of the Union address of January 1957, called on labor and business to exercise caution in wage and price policies; urged the conservation of the nation's natural resources; and exhorted people in all sections of the country to support him in moving closer to the goal of fair and equal treatment of citizens without regard to race or color. Given the revolution in civil rights that occurred during his administration, the president's comments in this respect amounted to classic understatement.

The Breakthrough in Race Relations

The modern civil rights movement gained momentum during the Eisenhower presidency, in particular after the celebrated United States Supreme Court decision in the case of *Brown* v. *Board of Education of Topeka* handed down on May 17, 1954. In a unanimous decision delivered by Chief Justice Earl Warren, an Eisenhower appointee, on behalf of a unanimous consensus, the Supreme Court reversed its ruling of 1896 of *Plessy* v. *Ferguson,* which sanctioned segregation of the races under the doctrine of "separate but equal." The Court upheld the plaintiff's contention that segregated public schools were not "equal" and could not be made "equal," and that hence they had been deprived of equal protection of the law. The highest court in the land faced the question squarely: "Does segregation of children in public schools solely on the basis of race, even though the physical facilities and other 'tangible' factors may be equal, deprive the children of the minority group of equal educational opportunities?" Finding in the affirmative, the Court held that the "segregation of white and colored children," mainly as "the policy of separating the races is usually interpreted as denoting the inferiority of the Negro group." The message to the American people was unequivocal: "We conclude that in the field of public education the doctrine of 'separate but equal' has no place."

In a ruling a year later, the Court ordered southern states to proceed with the desegregation of their school districts, "with all deliberate speed." The South's lower courts were entrusted with the responsibility of effecting these changes. Southern critics of desegregation fought with every weapon at their disposal, bringing intense pressure to bear on southern politicians, from the municipal to the Federal level. While some rode the high ground of states' rights to oppose "forced" integration, much of the opposition was of the ugly variety, up to and including threats of physical violence. The first black to register at the University of Alabama in early 1956 was driven from the campus by a mob of angry students, a scene to be repeated in Texas and Tennessee. A showdown was in the works.

Against a background of massive resistance in the Deep South, where not a single school had been integrated since the Supreme Court decision, a Federal district court in 1957 nullified an Arkansas court injunction prohibiting the school board from commencing integration beginning with senior high school students. On the eve of the fall semester at Little Rock's Central High School, Governor Orval E. Faubus called out the National Guard to maintain law and order there, a pretext aimed at *preventing* nine black students from attending classes. In spite of a meeting with the president at Newport, Rhode Island, in September, Governor Faubus failed to remove the Guard until he was served with a Federal injunction barring him from obstructing the entry of the black students. Shortly afterward, on September 23, violence broke out.

Though he had taken a Delphian position on the Supreme Court ruling of 1954—"I refused to say whether I either approved it or disapproved it"— President Eisenhower showed not the slightest hesitation in enforcing the letter of the law. Accordingly, on September 24, he dispatched one thousand paratroopers of the 101st Airborne Division from nearby Fort Campbell, Kentucky, and he federalized the Arkansas National Guard. Within days the black students were attending school under armed guard. The people of Arkansas responded by reelecting Governor Faubus who in turn brought the matter to the Supreme Court. In September 1958 the Court held its ground, declaring that "the constitutional rights [of the black children] are not to be sacrificed or yielded to the violence and disorder which have followed the actions of the [Arkansas] Governor and Legislature." Though further progress would be disappointingly slow, a start had at least been made.

On other matters, blacks took the lead in breaking down the dubious legal barriers and Jim Crow statutes that separated the races in the South. Segregated transportation came under fire when, on December 1, 1955, a forty-three-year-old black seamstress, Rosa Parks, refused to move to the designated "colored" section of a bus in Montgomery, Alabama; under the city's municipal segregation ordinance, blacks rode in the back of the bus while whites rode in the front. Thousands of blacks boycotted the bus company until the Supreme Court found in their favor in November; a month later unsegregated bus services commenced. The policy of passive resistance conferred the mantle of southern black leadership on a young Baptist minister, the Reverend Martin Luther King, Jr., while in the North, Roy

Wilkins of the National Association for the Advancement of Colored People and Floyd McKissick of the Congress on Racial Equality developed strategy there.

By the end of the Eisenhower era, sit-ins and freedom rides had broken down such discriminatory southern practices as segregated lunch counters and facilities on interstate highways. Moving in yet another direction, the administration's Civil Rights Acts of 1957 and of 1960 went a long way toward bringing southern Negroes closer to their ballot boxes by creating new voting rights protections. Like others, the laws' limitations became painfully obvious in the face of racial hostility and generations of conditioning. Still, the laws represented the most significant civil rights legislation since the days of Civil War Reconstruction.

The Eisenhower Doctrine

Although Moscow had shown that outright military conquest was not its method of operation in the Middle East, Washington feared that states under Soviet influence might resort to violence to extend the boundaries of communism; the principal objects of this fear were Egypt and Syria, both of which had developed strong ties with the Soviet bloc. To guard against possible incursions into the area, President Eisenhower secured from Congress, on March 9, 1957, a joint resolution setting forth what eventually came to be known as the Eisenhower Doctrine. Essentially, it empowered the president to use the armed forces of the United States, at the request of any nation in the Middle East, to protect it against overt armed aggression from any nation controlled by international communism. Though no nation of the region made the kind of request envisaged in the resolution, the administration found two occasions to act at least in the spirit of it. The first, a few weeks after the passage of the resolution, was on behalf of pro-Western King Hussein of Jordan, who was threatened by Egyptian and Syrian-supported leftist agitators. Among moves that included the showing of the American Sixth Fleet and a grant to Hussein of $30 million in economic and military aid, the situation brought forth from the president a declaration that he considered the independence of Jordan vital to American security.

The second occasion occurred in the wake of a violent revolution in Iraq in July 1958 when the king, the crown prince, and all friends of the West were assassinated. A new government—not communist, but friendly to the Soviet Union— took control and withdrew Iraq from the Baghdad Pact. The immediate Western reaction to the Iraq revolution was that it had been orchestrated by Nasser, who would then turn on Jordan and Lebanon. In Lebanon, in fact, there was already an armed rebellion in progress. After news of the Iraqi revolution, Lebanon and Jordan appealed for military protection to Washington and London respectively. Both appeals met swift response. The United States landed fourteen thousand marines and airborne troops in Lebanon as Britain landed three thousand paratroopers in Jordan. After the situation had quieted down, American troops were withdrawn from Lebanon in October, and the British left Jordan in November.

The most serious crisis in Soviet-American relations during the second Eisenhower administration concerned Berlin. In a speech in November 1958 and in a series of notes to Washington, London, and Paris, Khrushchev demanded an end to the occupation of West Berlin by the Western powers. He insisted upon a solution within six months, threatening otherwise to make a separate peace with East Germany and leave the Allies to negotiate their rights in Berlin and their access there with a government they did not recognize. In December, the Allies joined in an unqualified rejection of the Soviet ultimatum. Faced by a determined and unified West, Krushchev softened the tone of his demand by letting it be known that the six-month time limit was not to be taken literally. After two meetings of the Big Four foreign ministers in Geneva failed to make headway on the problem, President Eisenhower invited the Soviet leader to visit him at Camp David, his mountain retreat in Maryland. Their meeting there, on September 25–27, 1959, climaxed ten days in which Khrushchev's touring of America—including a trip to Disneyland—and his sensational proposal at the United Nations of general and complete disarmament dominated the media. Despite the so-called spirit of Camp David and an invitation to the president to visit the USSR the following spring, the troublesome Berlin question remained.

In December, after the Camp David meeting, the Western Allies proposed a summit meeting of the Big Four for the coming May in Paris. The Soviets accepted, with Eisenhower's visit to the Soviet Union to follow in June. Prospects of agreement on Berlin, growing dimmer in the months prior to the Paris meeting, were completely destroyed by Khrushchev's reaction to the U-2 incident that occurred early in May.

On May 1, a high-altitude United States reconnaissance plane of the U-2 type was shot down while on an espionage flight across the USSR from Pakistan to Norway. The pilot, Gary Powers, was captured unharmed, along with his photographic and other equipment. After some internal skirmishing, Eisenhower accepted reponsibility for such flights as a necessary safeguard against surprise attacks. The Kremlin seized upon the incident to wreck the summit conference, which ended abruptly on May 17, one day after its opening. The Soviet invitation to Eisenhower to visit the USSR was withdrawn.

Closer to home the administration witnessed the successful overthrow of Cuban dictator Fulgencio Batista on New Year's Day, 1959, by the bearded revolutionary Fidel Castro. Within a short period of time, Castro transformed his regime into one frankly communist, clearly affiliated with the communist bloc. Early promises of free elections and a free press were repudiated; foreign property, including American property worth $1 billion, was confiscated; and large-scale economic and military aid poured in from the Soviet Union. Cuba, in the administration's view, had become the fountainhead of communist propaganda and training school of revolutionaries for Latin America. For lack of regional support, Washington could only take unilateral action against Castro in retaliation for the latter's wholesale confiscation of American property and his continued propaganda abuse of the United States. In July 1960, President Eisenhower canceled about 95 percent of Cuba's remaining quota of sugar imports for the year, some months later canceling entirely the quota for the first quarter of 1961. An embargo on all shipments to Cuba save foodstuffs and medical supplies followed. And on January 3, 1961, the president cut off all diplomatic and consular traffic with Havana. The next move would be left to Eisenhower's successor.

The Military-Industrial Complex

Contemporary criticism of President Eisenhower ranged from the mild to the extreme. Disaffected speech writer Emmet John Hughes judged the Eisenhower years to be both a personal and political tragedy: personal in the sense that the president had the support and resources to bring about great changes and did not, and political in the sense that he possessed the strength to revitalize the two-party system and failed to do so. Critics of a more liberal persuasion judged Eisenhower lazy, tongue-twisted, and frankly out of his depth in the White House, "a five-star babe in the woods." By the mid 1970s, according to one student of the Eisenhower literature, the president appeared "to be a more astute and more sophisticated politician, a stronger and more concerned chief executive, a more successful president both in domestic and foreign affairs, a more prescient and imaginative leader and a more energetic, perceptive, and compassionate person." By the early 1980s, some Eisenhower revisionists had gone so far as to argue that he was a political genius, a master of "the hidden hand." What one could not gainsay were the basic facts that he managed to survive two terms in office without taking the United States into war and that he presided over a relatively prosperous economy while holding down inflation.

Sensitive to criticism of his "style" of leadership—or alleged lack of it—Eisenhower showed a keeness in defending his achievements in office. In a letter written in 1966 to his former press secretary James C. Hagerty, he listed his accomplishments to include, among others, the statehood of Alaska and Hawaii; the buiding of the St. Lawrence Seaway; the ending of the Korean War; the largest reduction of taxes to that time; the first civil rights law in eighty years; the containment of communism in Iran, Guatemala, Lebanon, Formosa, and South Vietnam; the initiation of the most amibitous interstate highway system in history; the launching of a space and a ballistic missle program; starting Federal medical care for the aged; and using executive power to enforce the order of a Federal court in Arkansas with no loss of life. Interestingly, the former president left off the one item for which most Americans have since come to remember him: his poignant warning of the danger of the military-industrial complex.

In his farewell address to the American people delivered on January 17, 1961, Eisenhower noted that the conjunction of an immense military establishment and a large arms industry, each in itself necessary, was new in the American experience. Recognizing the imperative need for this developement, he warned his fellow citizens that they must not fail to comprehend its grave implications. Specifically, he went on, "In the councils of government, we must guard against the acquisition of unwarranted influence whether sought or unsought, by the military-industrial complex. The potential for the disasterous rise of misplaced power exists and will persist." In the circumstances, the president concluded, "Only an alert and knowledgeable citizenry can compel the proper meshing of the huge industrial and military machinery of defence with our peaceful methods and goals, so that security and liberty may prosper together."

Eisenhower was a citizen as well as a soldier. Because of his experience in both the army and the presidency, he knew firsthand the connection between industrialists and bureaucrats. His message was clear; his remedy, less so.

Suggested Readings

Alexander, Charles C. *Holding the Line: The Eisenhower Era, 1952-1961*. 1975.
Cox, Archibald. *The Warren Court*. 1968.
Divine, Robert A. *Eisenhower and the Cold War*. 1980.

Donovan, Robert J. *Eisenhower: The Inside Story*. 1956.

Draper, Theodore. *Castro's Revolution*. 1962.

Duram, James C. *A Moderate among Extremists; Dwight D. Eisenhower and the School Desegration Crisis* 1981.

Eisenhower, Dwight D., *Mandate for Change*. 1963.

————. *Waging Peace*. 1965.

Ferrell, Robert H., ed. *The Eisenhower Diaries*. 1981.

————. *The Diary of James C. Hagerty: Eisenhower in Mid-Course, 1954–1955*. 1983.

Finer, Herman. *Dulles over Suez*. 1964.

Geelhoed, E. Bruce. *Charles E. Wilson and Controversy at the Pentagon, 1953-1957*. 1979.

Graebner, Norman A. *The New Isolationism*. 1956.

Greenstein, Fred I *The Hidden-Hand Presidency: Eisenhower as Leader*. 1982.

Hoopes, Townsend. *The Devil and John Foster Dulles*. 1973.

Hughes, Emmet John. *The Ordeal of Power: A Political Memoir of the Eisenhower Years*. 1963.

Huntington, Samuel P. *The Common Defense*. 1961.

King, Jr., Martin Luther. *Stride toward Freedom*. 1958.

Larson, Arthur. *A Republican Looks at his Party*. 1956.

Lewis, Anthony. *Portrait of a Decade: The Second American Revolution*. 1964.

Lubell, Samuel. *The Revolt of the Moderates*. 1956.

Neff, Donald. *Warriors at Suez*. 1981.

Nixon, Richard M. *Six Crises*. 1962.

Parmet, Herbert S. *Eisenhower and the American Crusades*. 1972.

Preussen, Ronald W. *John Foster Dulles: The Road to Power*. 1982.

Rae, J.B. *The Road and the Car in American Life*. 1971.

Reichard, Gary W. *The Reaffirmation of Republicanism*. 1975.

Rose, Mark H. *Interstate: Express Highway Politics, 1941-1956*. 1979.

3

John of a Thousand Days

The presidential election of 1960 marked the changing of the guard in the United States, bringing to the forefront the first generation of politicians to be born in the twentieth century. At the Democratic National Convention meeting in Los Angeles in early July, Senator John F. Kennedy, the cool young man from Massachusetts, swept a first-ballot nomination and, in the process, overwhelmed his nearest rival, Senator Lyndon B. Johnson of Texas, the Senate majority leader. Only forty-three years old in 1960, Kennedy was a cultured man of intellectual leanings, the scion of a well-known and wealthy Boston-Irish family. A Roman Catholic and a hero in World War II, Kennedy had served fourteen years in Congress, eight of them as the junior senator from Massachusetts.

To placate the South, which unsuccessfully resisted the adoption of the strongest civil rights planks in the party's history, Kennedy bypassed a number of leading personalities, including Senators Hubert Humphrey of Minnesota and Stuart Symington of Missouri, to select Johnson as his running mate. In addition to strong civil rights measures, the Democratic platform argued in favor of placing medical care for the aged under the auspices of the social security program and argued against the Eisenhower administration's tight-money policies.

Several weeks later at the Republican National Convention meeting in Chicago, Vice-President Richard Nixon also swept a first-ballot presidential nomination, having long beforehand eliminated the challenge of

Governor Nelson Rockefeller of New York who, nonetheless, influenced the domestic and foreign policy planks of the party platform. Nixon, the first vice-president in the history of the modern two-party system to win the nomination in his own right, then proceeded to choose Henry Cabot Lodge, chief United States delegate to the United Nations, as his vice-presidential running mate. For its part, the Republican party reaffirmed the policies and tone of the Eisenhower White House, pledging more funds for national defense, a contributory health program, and a stronger stand on civil rights. Of humbler origins than Kennedy, the forty-seven year old Nixon was born into a California Quaker family, attended public schools, received an undergraduate degree from Whittier College in 1937, and completed his law studies at Duke University three years later. After a brief stint with the Office of Price Administration, he served in the navy for four years, reaching the rank of lieutenant commander. From California Nixon was elected to the 80th Congress where he made his reputation in the notorious Alger Hiss investigation.

A Gallup poll in late August confirmed what most political analysts had already concluded: it was going to be a very close race. According to the poll, Nixon and Kennedy were tied at 47 percent each, with 6 percent undecided. As in most presidential campaigns, the personalities of the candidates weighed more heavily in the balance than the programs and the party platforms they espoused. Both were comparatively young; both possessed an inner ruthlessness. Neither had the comforting image that had swept General Eisenhower into office eight years before. Republican critics assailed the wealthy and Harvard-trained Kennedy as an irresponsible smart aleck, quoting former President Truman to the effect that Kennedy was not ready to be president and the country was not ready for him. Critics of candidate Nixon questioned both his credentials and his integrity; the majority of liberals simply did not like anything about him.

Perhaps the greatest imponderable was Kennedy's religion. The only other Roman Catholic to head the Democratic ticket, Al Smith, was swamped by Herbert Hoover in 1928. The "Catholic question" had been raised in the course of the West Virginia primary and would not go away. Accordingly, Kennedy met the issue head on, appearing before an influential gathering of Protestant ministers in Houston in September. "I believe in America," he told them, "where the separation of Church and State is absolute—where no Catholic prelate would tell the President (should he be a Catholic) how to act, and no Protestant minister would tell his parishioners for whom to vote—where no church or church school is granted any public funds or political preference—and where no man is denied public office merely because his religion differs from the President who might appoint him or the people who might elect him." By bringing the issue out in the open and answering his critics directly, Kennedy fully succeeded in neutralizing the religious question.

Particularly noteworthy were the four, face-to-face encounters between the candidates on national television in late September and October. In the first television debates of their kind—actually, newsmen questioned the candidates and they in turn were allowed to challenge each other's comments—the general feeling was that the telegenic Kennedy came out ahead; at the very least, he showed he could handle himself, though his aggressive attitude toward Cuba and the lack of support for the Nationalist Chinese–held islands of Quemoy and Matsu managed to irritate many. In particular, Nixon regarded Kennedy's call for American support of an anti-Castro revolution in Cuba as dangerously irresponsible and shockingly reckless, contrary to the nation's treaty commitments with Latin America and its obligations under the United Nations Charter. The vice-president advocated instead an economic "quarantine" of Cuba. Other presidential issues dealt with matters of Soviet-American relations, United States prestige abroad, education, and welfare.

After a strenuous campaign, which included thousands of miles of travel on both sides, Senator Kennedy won the election from Vice-President Nixon by the astonishing margin of just over 100,000 votes out of a record of 68.8 million votes cast, a plurality of less than .05 percent of the total vote. This was the smallest percentage difference in the popular vote category of two presidential candidates since 1880; put another way, the margin amounted to less than two votes per voting precinct. The final count showed the cool young man from Massachusetts receiving 34,229,731 votes (49.9 percent) and his opponent 34,108,157 (49.6 percent). The electoral column was a different story with a Kennedy margin of 303 to 219, and even here the results could have been reversed if only 11,869 voters in five states had voted the other way. At most Kennedy's religion cost him 2 percent of the total popular vote but was probably the key factor in swaying blocs of Catholic voters (78 percent) and sympathetic minority groups in crucial industrial states where a great number of electoral votes were at stake. Kennedy was himself convinced that "it was T.V. more than anything else that turned the tide."

The election of John Kennedy broke a number of precedents. For one thing, at forty-three years old, he was the youngest man ever elected to the presidency; for another, he was the first Roman Catholic to win the office. And for good measure, the Democrats retained control of Congress, though with slightly reduced margins. Divided government in Washington came abruptly to an end, yet Republicans and southern Democrats in Congress (the conservative coalition) still outnumbered moderate and liberal Democrats, not to mention southern domination of committees in Congress because of the seniority system.

As early as his acceptance speech at Los Angeles, Kennedy made it clear that his goal was to "get the country moving again." Americans he said, stood "on the edge of a New Frontier—the frontier of the 1960s—a frontier of unknown opportunities and perils—a frontier of unfilled hopes and threats." His purpose was to offer the nation a set of challenges that appealed to its pride. In this regard he envisaged the White House as the national center of action, with the president actively leading the country and the Congress. Furthermore, what could not be accomplished by legislative action might just as well be accomplished by executive action.

Few could argue that the American people had given the senator from Massachusetts anything like a clear mandate. Even American blacks were not quite certain what to make of him, despite Kennedy's late-October phone call to Mrs. Martin Luther King, Jr. concerning the recent jailing of her husband in connection with a demonstration to end racial segregation in Atlanta's department stores. (That the president's brother Robert managed to arrange bail for Dr. King—the most influential symbol of the sit-in movement— must certainly have raised hopes.)

In any case, in his inaugural address several months later, on January 20, 1961, the president spelled out his challenge to the American people in unequivocal terms. "We observe today," he told his audience on the bright winter day, "not a victory of party but a celebration of freedom—symbolizing an end as well as a beginning—signifying renewal as well as change." Asking his fellow countrymen to remember their own revolutionary origins, he continued:

Let the word go forth from this time and place, to friend and foe alike, that the torch has been passed to a new generation of Americans—born in this century, tempered by war, disciplined by a hard and bitter peace, proud of our ancient heritage, and unwilling to witness or permit the slow undoing of those human rights to which this nation has always been committed, and to which we are committed today at home and around the world.

Let every nation know, whether it wishes us well or ill, that we shall pay any price, bear any burden, meet any hardship, support any friend, oppose any foe to assure the survival and success of liberty.

From the Soviet Union, to which he referred as "our adversary," the president called for an exploration of the problems that united the superpowers rather than the ones that divided them. In this sense, he observed, "Let us never negotiate out of fear. But let us never fear to negotiate."

To achieve these goals, Kennedy surrounded himself with liberal intellectuals espousing the belief that technology and social planning could overcome any problem, and remake any society into the image and likeness of the United States. For his secretary of state the president selected Dean Rusk, a former assistant secretary of state in the Truman administration and president of the Rockefeller Foundation since 1952; for secretary of defense, Robert S. McNamara, a former president of the Ford Motor Company; and for national security adviser, McGeorge Bundy, from the East Coast academic establishment. For attorney general, Kennedy chose his own brother Robert, ten years his junior. And so it went. A stream of young, rich, and professional elite poured into Washington, each to add to the tone of a White House unafraid to play host to the best and the brightest. Enhancing this image was the president's elegant wife, Jacqueline, and their energetic family. Surely, this was an administration poised to "get the country moving again."

The Bay of Pigs

The Latin American aid program launched in the closing months of the Eisenhower administration was taken over by President Kennedy in his Alliance for Progress (*Alianza para el Progreso*). Essentially, the president envisaged a ten-year plan of economic development and social progress and reform—a sort of Marshall Plan for Latin America. Without mentioning figures, Secretary of the Treasury Douglas Dillon, speaking at an Inter-American Economic and Social Conference at Punta del Este, Uruguay, in August estimated that at least $20 billion could be available from outside sources—North America, Europe, and Japan—during the next decade, mostly from public agencies. The conferees then proceeded to adopt a charter defining the aims and procedures of the Alliance for Progress and a "Declaration of the Peoples of America," both signed on August 17, 1961. For its part, Washington pledged to provide a major part of the $20 billion, principally in public funds. Cuba was represented at Punta del Este by its leading communist theoretician, Che Guevara, who did not sign the charter. Furthermore, Secretary Dillon made it clear that Cuba could expect no aid from the United States as long as it remained under communist rule.

Despite the fanfare the Alliance for Progess got off to a disappointingly slow start. Two years after its inauguration at Punta del Este, the United

States had committed a total of $2.1 billion to the program and had disbursed over $1.5 billion, mainly for such items as residential housing, hospitals and schools; overall, it made a relatively small contribution to the self-sustaining economic growth on which the eventual success of the program would depend. Private capital tended, moreover, to be frightened away by political insecurity. Entrenched resistance to reforms in landholding and taxation similarly took their toll, adding little to the promotion of political democracy in the Western Hemisphere. In many ways, the volunteer Peace Corps, bringing ordinary Americans to work side by side with ordinary people in villages and elsewhere in Latin America and other underdeveloped parts of the world, may have had a more lasting impact than formal proclamations, charters, or showcase structures.

In addition to the Cuban problem, Eisenhower had handed over to the young president a secret plan to deal with the troublesome Fidel Castro. By the spring of 1960, it had been decided to sponsor an invasion of Cuba by anti-Castro refugees of which there seemed to be no end. President Kennedy soon endorsed the plan himself, assured by his own military advisers and the Central Intelligence Agency that the probable chance of success was good. In the early hours of April 17, 1961, an "army" of approximately two thousand Cuban refugees landed at Bahia de Cochinos (Bay of Pigs) on Cuba's southern coast. In the absence of American air cover, which the exiles anticipated, the army of refugees found itself quickly overwhelmed by Castro's forces. The expected popular uprising, which American intelligence confidently predicted, failed to materialize. The result was a fiasco and an embarrassment to the administration.

To a message from Moscow threatening all-out war if the United States should invade Cuba, President Kennedy replied that America intended no military invasion but made it clear that, in the event of outside military intervention, he would honor existing obligations under the inter-American system to protect the Western Hemisphere against external aggression.

As for Castro, he was strengthened and emboldened by his success in crushing the invasion and by cracking down on those suspected of disloyalty at home. In the following year he called for a continental civil war to topple governments in Latin America.

To the Cuban Missile Crisis

With the settlement of the German issue much in his mind, Khrushchev looked forward to dealing with a Democrat in the White House, for it was plain that he hoped to find Eisenhower's successor more yielding. In June

1961 Chairman Khrushchev and President Kennedy met for a two-day conference in Vienna. Although the meeting was superficially cordial and businesslike, Khrushchev managed to resurrect the Berlin crisis on much the same terms as before—and, again, with a six-month time limit. Unless the four occupying powers could agree on a peace treaty or treaties with Germany within that time, the Kremlin would conclude a separate treaty with East Germany and would terminate access rights to West Berlin. The future of West Berlin would be much in doubt.

In July, Kennedy responded that the United States and its allies would not allow the communists to drive them out of Berlin, a city of two million people living in freedom. Remarking that "we do not want to fight, but we have fought before," the president asked Congress for a $3.2 billion increase in the defense budget, for an increase in military manpower, and for authority to activate various reserve units. By increasing conventional forces at home and abroad, the president sought to broaden his options; in his words, "to have a wider choice than humiliation or all-out nuclear action." While thousands of Americans built fallout shelters, being less confident of presidential options than the commander in chief, Congress gave Kennedy everything for which he asked.

As part of the strategy, an additional forty-five thousand troops were moved to Europe. This, together with a French and West German build-up in NATO forces, brought the Western alliance up to twenty-five divisions. The Soviets canceled their time limit, but constructed a wall separating East from West Berlin, thus ending West Berlin's important role as an escape hatch from communist East Germany. Washington responded by protest only.

At the end of August, Khrushchev initiated a new series of nuclear tests in the atmosphere, ending an informal moratorium begun in 1958. By the end of the year, the Kremlin publicly announced a large increase in its defense budget. It appeared that Chairman Krushchev had badly underestimated the resolve of his youthful rival in the West. In this acrimonious atmosphere, the Cold War dangerously threatened to heat up.

On the evening of Monday, October 22, 1962, President Kennedy made the startling disclosure that a series of Soviet missile sites were in preparation on the island of Cuba. Their purpose, he explained to a spellbound nation, could be "none other than to provide a nuclear strike capability against the Western Hemisphere." Some of the sites were designed for medium-range ballistic missiles with a range of over a thousand miles; others not yet completed appeared to be designed for intermediate-range missiles with a capability of reaching as far as Hudson's Bay, Canada, to the north, or Lima, Peru, to the south.

In the address in which he denounced the cloak of secrecy and deception under which the missiles had been spirited into Cuba, President Kennedy voiced a grave warning to the Kremlin: In future, the United States would "regard any nuclear missile launched from Cuba against any nation in the Western Hemisphere as an attack by the Soviet Union on the United States requiring a full retaliatory response upon the Soviet Union." Let Chairman Khrushchev, he urged, "halt and eliminate this clandestine, reckless and provocative threat to world peace and to stable relations between our two nations."

Meanwhile, the administration called for a strict quarantine of all offensive military equipment under shipment to Cuba; a continued and increased close surveillance of Cuba; a reinforced American base at Guantanamo Bay; an immediate meeting of the Organization of American States to consider this latest threat to hemispheric security; and asked that an emergency meeting of the Security Council be convoked without delay to consider what action might be taken to preserve the peace. The world thus witnessed the first major crisis of the nuclear age—the first eyeball-to-eyeball confrontation between the superpowers, to paraphrase Secretary of State Dean Rusk. The question remained, Who would blink first?

The blockade or "quarantine" was scheduled to go into effect on Wednesday morning. On Tuesday Rusk convened the Council of the Organization of American States and secured an overwhelming vote in support of the American position. The adopted resolution called for the immediate dismantling and withdrawal from Cuba of all missiles and other weapons with any offensive capability and the taking of all necessary measures, including force, to prevent the further arming of Cuba by the Sino-Soviet powers. This unanimous endorsement of the blockade of Cuba by the OAS, which provided the legal basis for Kennedy's strategy, was given under the authority of the Rio Treaty of Reciprocal Assistance of 1947.

The world literally held its breath. Washington, with the support of the OAS and its major European allies, had reacted with resolute firmness to an unexpected threat to its security and that of the hemisphere. It was the Soviets who "blinked first" with some assistance from Secretary-General U. Thant of the United Nations.

Khruschchev did not challenge the blockade. Some Soviet ships en route to Cuba voluntarily turned back; others, known to be carrying inoffensive cargoes, were allowed to proceed. In a series of complex exchanges with the president, which lasted until Sunday, October 28, Khruschchev agreed to withdraw the missiles in question and a number of long-range bombers and to see to dismantling the missile sites. In return for these concessions (whose implementation was to be subject to international inspection), Kennedy promised that the United States would not invade Cuba.

While the matter remained complicated because of Castro's veto power over any international inspection, Kennedy was satisfied that the missiles and bombers had in fact been removed and the sites dismantled according to agreement. In any event, thousands of Soviet troops and technicians stayed in Cuba after the crisis. Cuba continued to be a communist state under the Soviet aegis and a training center and base for communists operating elsewhere in the hemisphere.

In terms of nuclear arms control, the Cuban Missile Crisis produced major yet contradictory effects. It provided renewed momentum for arms control as both Moscow and Washington recognized that they might not be so fortunate next time. After discovering the difficulty of communication in times of crises, the White House and the Kremlin negotiated the so-called Hot Line agreement, signed in July 1963, providing for special crisis-communication facilities between the superpowers. More significantly, in July the United States and the Soviet Union, together with Great Britain, concluded the Partial Nuclear Test Ban Treaty, which prohibited nuclear testing in the atmosphere, in outer space, and under water. This treaty has correctly been cited as the first real success in limiting the arms race.

On the negative side of the ledger, the crisis provided impetus for yet another escalation in the arms race. Policy makers in the Soviet Union, not unreasonably, concluded from their Cuban experience that ICBM superiority provided the critical edge in diplomatic bargaining and resolved to enlarge their strategic arsenal both in qualitative and quantitative terms. During the mid- and late-sixties, the Kremlin substantially increased its defense expenditures for offensive and defensive strategic weapons systems. Accordingly, a succession of new ICBMs entered the Soviet Strategic Rocket Forces; by 1970, the USSR managed to surpass the United States in operational ICBMs (1,100 to 1,054), though America still possessed more separate warheads.

The arms control approach dominated the Arms Control and Disarmament Agency created by President Kennedy in September 1961 at the urging of John J. McCloy, assistant secretary of war during World War II. Yet it was not arms control but an acceleration in strategic weapons development and deployment that first characterized the administration. The acceleration, instituted as part of a larger defense formula known as "flexible response," paradoxically implied a reduction in the importance of nuclear reliance.

Under this formula the primary function of America's strategic force was to deter the opponent's use of his own. Below this level, nonnuclear forces would be employed to resist what aggression could not be prevented with nuclear deterrence, thus providing the rationale for increased and upgraded American conventional forces to permit the president to respond "flexibly."

Despite both the renewed emphasis on conventional forces and the discovery by Secretary of Defense McNamara that the "missile gap" was an illusion—the United States had all along had a four-to-one superiority in long-range strategic weapons over the Soviet Union—the expansion in America's missile program was not slowed. In the early 1960s, the nation's first-generation ICBMs (Atlas-E, Atlas-F, and Titan-I) became fully operational, while work on second-generation missiles (Minuteman-I and Titan-II) began. After the Cuban crisis, in contrast to the Soviet buildup, the United States decreased its proportionate expenditure on nuclear forces, leveling off on the number of missiles deployed on land and on submarines.

McNamara, subsequently regretting the earlier decision to accelerate, determined upon nuclear sufficiency rather than superiority as the proper objective. Defining sufficiency as the capacity to emerge from a Soviet surprise attack with sufficient forces in reserve to devastate the Soviet Union in a second strike, McNamara saw it as a stabilizing factor guaranteeing mutual deterrence but avoiding the necessity of superfluous weapons; throughout the remainder of the 1960s McNamara concentrated on developing a cost-effective nuclear force structure to maintain this second-strike capability.

The Road to Vietnam

The Geneva settlement of 1954 had left Laos' communist forces, the Pathet Lao (Lao nation) in occupation of two northeastern provinces adjoining North Vietnam and the People's Republic of China. Attempts by the neutralist faction to integrate these forces and their leaders into the Laotian army and government invariably aroused rightist opposition. Successive attempts by the Pathet Lao led to armed resistance, putatively supported by communist regulars from Hanoi. A civil war between the left and the right threatened to escalate into a major conflict between Washington and Moscow: the United States, which had assumed the task of training and supplying the Royal Laotian Army, aided the right while the Soviet Union aided the communists. As the Royal Army proved unequal to the communist offensive, it became increasingly apparent in Washington that only some kind of intervention from the outside world could preserve even a semblance of a neutral Laos.

Its efforts stimulated by the joint statement of President Kennedy and Premier Khrushchev made at their Vienna summit reaffirming their support of a neutral and independent Laos, a fourteen-nation conference met at Geneva in May 1961. The only neutralist solution for Laos, all agreed, was to be found in a coalition government representative of Laos' three main factions. Agreement among them required a year of hard bargaining, during which time yet another communist offensive in the region threatened to spill over into Thailand, a SEATO ally of the United States. (The landing in Thailand of eighteen hundred marines from the Seventh Fleet, followed by token forces from Britain, Australia, and New Zealand, headed off any such danger and probably expedited a Laotian settlement.) By June 1962 a coalition had been constructed, with the new government committed to neutrality and nonentanglement in any alliance of military coalition (i.e., SEATO). The transaction was completed at Geneva on July 21, 1962, when the fourteen nations of the conference signed the documents and agreed to respect the independence, sovereignty, neutrality, and territorial integrity of the Kingdom of Laos while setting forth rules for an international commission that presumably was to supervise the settlement. Intermittent pressure by communist forces upon neutralist and rightist elements made it plain that the Laotion settlement would never be more than a shaky armistice waiting for trouble. In any case, in the matter of Vietnam, the administration proved much less inclined to compromise.

Kennedy had been in office only a few months when he received an appeal for increased military spending from President Ngo Dinh Diem of South Vietnam. For the past several years Diem's government had been engaged in a guerilla war with the Viet Cong, who had established their control of many rural areas. Whether this conflict was a war of aggression by the North against the South, or a genuine civil war with Ho Chi Minh of North Vietnam coming to the aid of his communist brethren, there could be little doubt that guerilla warfare was erupting all over Vietnam. To make matters worse, American military advisers provided the native army with training only for a conventional war based on the Korean model, while political advisers were unable to persuade Diem to adopt reforms that might have rallied the peasantry.

In December of 1960, the formation of the National Liberation Front of South Vietnam was announced. Designed as the political arm of the movement in which the Viet Cong were the military, the NLF clearly seems to have owed its inspiration to Hanoi. By 1969 southerners who had withdrawn to the north at the time of partition, flooded back to the south and joined the resistance. By this time the Viet Cong had extended their influence to much of the South Vietnamese countryside.

It was in these circumstances that Kennedy sent Vice-President Lyndon B. Johnson on a fact-finding mission to Vietnam and elsewhere in Asia. Johnson, who as Senate Majority Leader had opposed intervention to save Dienbienphu in 1954, found the communist threat in Vietnam serious, echoing President Eisenhower's famous "domino theory." President Diem, it should be noted, did not at this time ask for U.S. troops. According to General Maxwell D. Taylor, whom Kennedy had sent on a similar mission a few months earlier, Diem would particularly welcome American personnel to assist in logistics and communications. Accepting the proposition that the terrorist campaigns were orchestrated by Hanoi in violation of the Geneva settlement, Kennedy promised to increase American assistance.

Now began a new phase of United States aid to South Vietnam, which for the period from 1955 to 1962 exceeded $2 billion and by 1963 approached the rate of $500 million annually. A dramatic indicator of the Kennedy policy was the arrival at Saigon, on December 12, 1961, of an American escort carrier bearing helicopters, training planes, and requisite crews numbering about four hundred men. This event served as the prelude to the so-called helicopter war in which American personnel were to participate throughout the next three years by flying Vietnamese troops over jungles and rice fields in an attempt to seek out the Viet Cong or communist guerillas.

In addition, the United States had undertaken to train the Vietnamese in antiguerilla tactics and had persuaded the Diem regime to launch a program isolating the peasantry from the Viet Cong by resettling them in fortified villages—a technique the British had found successful in fighting communists in Malaya. Persuaded that Vietnam represented "the cornerstone of the Free World in Southeast Asia, the Keystone of the arch, the finger in the dike, President Kennedy steadily expanded the American presence there. The number of United States "advisers" in Vietnam rose from 650 when Eisenhower left office to 16,500 before the end of 1963. By May 1964 more than 200 Americans had been killed (about half of them in battle). Since the beginning of the Kennedy program, a large number of American planes had also been shot down.

The administration's task was made even more difficult by a growing rift between non-Communist elements in the population and President Diem, whose government was in reality a shambles. Spurred on by his family and intolerant of criticism from any quarter, Diem resented

Washington's suggestions for alleviating popular discontent. Meanwhile, the war against the Viet Cong dragged on with no end in sight. Dissatisfaction with Diem reached a crisis point in the summer and fall of 1963. With the writing clearly on the wall—and with (probably) the tacit consent of the State Department—on November 1 a group of army officers overthrew the government and killed Diem. Kennedy promptly recognized the new provisional government, hoping for a more united and renewed effort against the Viet Cong.

The New Frontier

The New Frontier was launched in the depths of the fourth major recession since World War II. "We take office," observed President Kennedy in his message to Congress on January 30, 1960 (after little more than a week in office), "in the wake of seven months of recession, three and one-half years of slack, seven years of diminished economic growth, and nine years of falling farm income." To make matters worse, business bankruptcies had reached the highest level since the 1930s, farm incomes had been squeezed 25 percent since 1951 and 5.5 million people were looking for work. The economy was in trouble.

Essentially, the Kennedy economic program consisted of protecting the unemployed, of increasing the minimum wage, of lowering taxes, and of stimulating the economy, particularly in the business and housing sectors. Like most presidents, Kennedy met with stiff opposition from Congress. In 1961 the administration managed to expand social security benefits. The minimum wage was increased in stages to reach to $1.25 per hour, benefiting more than 27 million workers. Nearly $5 billion was allocated for an omnibus housing bill. More controversial was the Area Redevelopment Act, which authorized loans, grants, and technical assistance to depressed industrial and rural areas. As a consequence of pumping money into the economy both by domestic and military spending, the recession faded by the end of the president's first year in office.

In 1962 Kennedy's legislative program met with mixed results. On the positive side of the ledger, the president requested and received intact the Trade Expansion Act. Pronounced the most significant international economic legislation since the Marshall Plan, the Act gave him authority to negotiate for the reduction and removal of tariffs, as well as creating a new program of "adjustment assistance" aid to industries and workers especially hard hit by competitive imports. Congress also enacted an accelerated Public

Works Act and the Manpower Retraining Bill. The Communications Satellite Act, which authorized a privately owned and financed corporation, was also enacted in 1962.

Committed to "landing a man on the moon and returning him safely to earth" before the decade was out (realized in July 1969), Kennedy obtained increased appropriations for the National Aeronautics and Space Administration (NASA) and supported the U.S. manned space flight program to the hilt. In February 1962, Lieutenant Colonel John H. Glenn became the first American to orbit the earth, following the Soviet actions of Yuri Gagarin the previous May.

Closer to home, and on the negative side of the ledger, the administration's legislative program found rough sledding in the Congress. Its social welfare, agricultural, and civil rights proposals met strong opposition from southern as well as northern conservatives—including the powerful American Medical Association, which assailed national health insurance as little more than "socialized medicine." Several significant pieces of welfare legislation, however, did see the light of day. Among these were the Higher Education Facilities Act, which authorized a five-year Federal program for the growth and continuation or improvement of public and private higher education facilities; the Drug Industry Act, which established additional safeguards in the processing and prescription of drugs; and aid for research into mental illness and retardation.

There can be no question that the president gave much thought and energy to the problem of inflation. For, "If," in his words, "recession is . . . one enemy of a free economy—inflation is the other." Kennedy firmly believed that the first line of defense against inflation was the good sense and public spirit of business and labor working together to keep their total increases in profits and wages in line with productivity. According to the administration, the nation's basic national security policy rested on a "wage-price-productivity" triangle, the stability of which affected America's ability to grow economically, to export competitively, and to provide an adequate defense and foreign policy.

Against this background it is easy to understand the president's anger when United States Steel Corporation, the nation's preeminent producer, suddenly announced price increases averaging $6 a ton on April 10, 1962, only five days after the company had signed a new two-year, "noninflationary" contract with the United Steelworkers of America. The Kennedy administration had spent almost a year persuading both sides to exercise restraint. Feeling betrayed, the president accused the major steel corporations (five other big steel companies moved in step with U.S.

Steel the next day) of "irresponsible defiance" of the public interest and of "ruthless disregard" for the common good.

Roger M. Blough, chairman of the U. S. Steel Corporation, remonstrated with the argument that the increases amounted to no more than a partial "catch-up" adjustment, a mere three-tenths of a cent per pound. The president, who recalled his father's words "that all businessmen were sons-of-bitches, but I never believed it till now," swung into action, using all the power of his office to force a rollback. In addition to denouncing the companies involved, the White House announced the opening of grand jury proceedings leading to possible antitrust action and threatened to divert Federal purchasing orders to companies that had not raised prices. After seventy-two hours of this kind of pressure, combined with the decision by several other large companies not to proceed further, U.S. Steel Corporation backed down and rescinded the increase. The president had proved his point, but business criticism of the administration reached an intensity not seen since the New Deal days of Franklin Roosevelt.

Cribbed and confined by opponents of civil rights legislation in Congress, President Kennedy made extensive use of executive powers to improve the plight of blacks, particularly those facing difficulties in the Deep South. Interstate transportation systems with their related terminals were effectively desegregated. A number of blacks were appointed to high office, most notably Thurgood Marshall to the U.S. Circuit Court, Carl Rowan as ambassador to Finland, and Robert Weaver to the Housing and Home Financing Agency. Through the president's Committee on Equal Employment chaired by Vice-President Johnson, the administration succeeded, in part, in combating racial discrimimation in the employment policies of firms holding government contracts. Also, much effort went into strengthening the basic rights of blacks to vote, mainly in southern states that employed literacy tests and poll taxes. Robert Kennedy led the way in the area of voting reform, bringing over fifty suits in four states on behalf of blacks seeking to cast their ballots. And, finally, the Executive Order of Novembr 20, 1962, went a long—though imperfect—way toward eliminating racial (as well as religious) discrimination in housing financed with Federal aid. In these as in other cases involving racial discrimination, persuasion sometimes worked; other times, it did not.

In January 1961, black Mississippian James Meredith, a veteran of eight years in the United States Air Force, applied for admission to the University of Mississippi, where no black had ever been enrolled; his application was rejected on the grounds that the Negro school from which he was attempting to transfer was not properly accredited, and that his application lacked letters of recommendation from five alumni of "Ole Miss." In May Meredith filed suit in the United States District Court of Appeals for southern Mississippi, contending that his admission had been denied squarely on racial grounds. Sixteen months later, in the fall of 1962, the Federal courts ordered Meredith's admission.

The governor of Mississippi, Ross Barnett, a states' righter and white supremacist, chose to defy the order and bar enrollment. Knowing that there would come a time when, to quote candidate Kennedy, "The next President of the United States cannot stand above the battle engaging in vague little sermons on brotherhood," the White House tried persuasion with Barnett, federalized the Mississippi National Guard, and ordered an escort of Federal marshals to accompany Meredith to the campus. On October 1, 1962, Meredith was allowed to enroll during an ugly riot that took thousands of guardsmen and soldiers fifteen hours to quell. Hundreds were injured and two died, including a French journalist who said in his last article, "The Civil War has never ended." Meredith was graduated the next year.

By the spring of 1963, the civil rights movement together with broadly based support for black equality took on life of its own. Both the North and the South witnessed civil rights demonstrations on a massive scale. Led by Dr. Martin Luther King, Jr., blacks had reached the point where, "We're through with tokenism and gradualism. . . . We can't wait any longer." Slowly, inexorably, racial barriers came down in the hotels, universities, and recreational facilities of southern cities.

Where progress or even the prospect of progress seemed distant, blacks marched in the streets. In Birmingham, Alabama, King and his followers were met by the stereotypical southern police chief, in this instance "Bull" Connor, complete with cattle prods, police dogs, and fire hoses. Nothing could have been better calculated to bring the Kennedy administration into the foreground of the struggle for racial equality. When the governor of the State of Alabama, George C. Wallace, threatened to bar the entry of black students to the University of Alabama, he met the same fate as Governor Barnett of Mississippi, as Kennedy once again federalized the state National Guard. Moving a step further, the administration called on Congress to enact comprehensive legislation to protect and guarantee blacks their basic rights, measures supported by a huge "March on Washington" in June 1963, with a quarter of a million people in attendance. Unlike Eisenhower, Kennedy gave the marchers his moral support and left no one in doubt about his administration's position. But still, the president could not force the Congress to enact his legislative program, nor could he prevent the senseless murder of the leader of the Mississippi branch of the National Association for the Advancement of Colored People, Medgar Evers, or the killing of four children in a bomb attack on a Birmingham church in September 1963. In the same year the Reverend King admitted that while Kennedy had probably done a little more than his predecessor, the plight of the overwhelming majority of blacks remained the same.

Death in Dallas

On November 22, 1963, while riding through downtown Dallas in a motorcade, President Kennedy was shot and killed by an assassin, later identified as Lee Harvey Oswald. Oswald, who had once defected to the Soviet Union and had been active in the pro-Castro Fair Play for Cuba Committee, was subsequently arrested by Dallas police after a brief struggle in a nearby theater prior to which a policeman had also been slain. Within thirty minutes of the shooting, seventy-five million Americans had heard the news; by late afternoon ninety million Americans, or 99.8 percent of the adult population, had heard of the president's death. "It had been the greatest simultaneous experience in the history of their or any other people," wrote William Manchester.

There then followed a bizarre turn of events. While still in police custody, Oswald was himself shot and killed by an obscure Dallas nightclub owner, Jack Ruby, the whole drama of which was captured on national television. Theories of conspiracies filled the air. The official Warren Report, the study of the presidential commission headed by Chief Justice Earl Warren in 1964, concluded that Oswald alone killed President Kennedy and that there was no conspiracy. The commission also found that Ruby acted alone in killing Oswald.

Immediately after his assassination, President Kennedy was linked with Abraham Lincoln in the pantheon of great presidents. More than twenty years later JFK's popularity among Americans continues despite the various historical assessments that range from the stricken knight from the legends of Camelot and King Arthur of the 1960s to the Cold War image of the 1970s to the more complex political personality of the 1980s. There was pure tragedy in the death of someone of such style, wit, and grace at the hands, it appeared to most, of someone so lacking in these qualities.

It is now known that the "best and the brightest" were not generally the wisest. The prelude to the Cuban Missile Crisis was, after all, the disaster at the Bay of Pigs, prompted by paranoia within an immature administration.

And the revelation that the king of Camelot had questionable morals has further tended to tarnish what remains of the shining myth. What would he have accomplished had he lived longer? What history is left with, to quote the French ambassador of that time, is "a brilliant maybe."

In any case, as the nation mourned the loss of its youthful leader, a very different kind of man assumed the reins of power.

Suggested Readings

Allison, Graham T. *The Essence of Decision*. 1971.

Brauer, Carl M. *John Kennedy and the Second Reconstruction*. 1977.

Burns, James MacGregor. *John Kennedy: A Political Profile*. 1959.

Dinerstein, Herbert S. *The Making of a Missile Crisis: October 1962*. 1976.

FitzSimons, Louise. *The Kennedy Doctrine*. 1972.

Heath, Jim F. *Kennedy and the Business Community*. 1969.

Hilsman, Roger. *To Move a Nation: The Politics and Foreign Policy in the Administration of John F. Kennedy*. 1964.

Kern, Montagnet al. *The Kennedy Crisis: The Press, The Presidency, and Foreign Policy*. 1984.

Manchester, William. *Death of a President*. 1967.

Miroff, Bruce. *Pragmatic Illusions: The Presidential Politics of John F. Kennedy*. 1976.

Navasky, V.S. *Kennedy Justice*. 1971.

Neustadt, Richard E. *Presidential Power* (rev. ed.) 1969.

Paper, Lewis J. *The Promise and the Performance: The Leadership of John F. Kennedy*. 1975.

Parmet, Herbert S. *Jack: The Struggle of John F. Kennedy*. 1980.

————. *J.F.K.—The Presidency of John F. Kennedy*. 1983.

Rogers, W.D. *The Twilight Struggle: The Alliance for Progress and the Politics of Development in Latin America*. 1967.

Salinger, Pierre. *With Kennedy*. 1966

Schlesinger, Arthur M. *A Thousand Days*. 1965.

————. *The Bitter Heritage*. 1967.

Seaborg, Glenn T. *Kennedy, Khruschev and the Test Ban*. 1982.

Sorenson, Theodore C. *Kennedy*. 1965.

Sundquist, James L. *Politics and Policy*. 1968.

Walton, Richard J. *Cold War and Counter-Revolution*. 1972.

Weissman, Stephen. *American Foreign Policy in the Congo, 1960–1964*. 1974.

White, Theodore H. *The Making of the President, 1960*. 1961.

Wills, Garry. *The Kennedy: A Shattered Illusion*. 1982.

Zinn, Howard. *SNCC: The New Abolitionists*. 1964.

4

The Crippled Giant: Lyndon Johnson and the Great Society

Vice-President Lyndon Johnson, who had been riding in the third car in the fateful Dallas motorcade, was sworn in as the thirty-sixth president of the United States within two hours of the assassination. In contrast to the privileged upbringing of his predecessor, the fifty-five year old Johnson had come to prominence in Washington via a very different kind of route. The new president was born in 1908 in a three-room house, in poor farming country near Stonewall, Texas. The impoverished Texan worked his way through Southwest State Teachers College in San Marcos and afterward taught speech and debating in the Houston public school system. Working as state director of the National Youth Administration in the mid-1930s, Johnson's big break came in 1937 when he was elected to fill a congressional vacancy. With a brief leave of absence for naval duty in 1941–1942, he served in the House of Representatives until 1949; from that time until his selection as Kennedy's vice-president, Johnson served with distinction in the United States Senate, finally attaining the position of majority leader in 1955, an acknowledged master of the art of legislative persuasion.

Throughout his political career Johnson remained a staunch defender of the New and Fair Deals, with a commitment to the common welfare and an appeal to the middle ground of American political life. Large, irrepressible and homey in manner, the president possessed a reputation as a consummate politician. He also had a legendary appetite for gossip and an earthy sense of humor. (According to economist John Kenneth Galbraith, Johnson once observed of House Republican minority leader Gerald Ford, a former college football player with a problem knee, that he could not fart and chew gum at the same time.) In any case, and after a generation of concentration on problems of the Cold War, President Johnson made it clear that he was reviving the tradition of domestic reform.

The Kennedy Legacy

In his first State of the Union message to Congress, delivered on January 8, 1964, Lyndon Johnson showed every sign of carrying forward the plans and programs of John Fitzgerald Kennedy—"Not," Johnson said, "because of our sorrow or sympathy, but because they are right." In addition to retaining his predecessor's cabinet, LBJ guided two, key pieces of Kennedy's legislative program through to fruition. The first was the Tax Reduction Act, in February; the second, the Civil Rights Law of 1964, in July.

In the tax law, which was designed to stimulate the economy, personal income tax rates were reduced from a 20–91 percent scale to a 14–70 percent scale over a two-year period, while corporate tax rates were reduced from 52 to 48 percent. The civil rights law was the most far-reaching civil rights legislation since the era of Reconstruction. It prohibited discrimination in areas of public accommodation, publicly owned facilities, employment, union membership, and federally aided programs. It also authorized the attorney general to institute suits to desegregate schools or other public facilities, and it outlawed discrimination in employment on the basis of race, color, religion, sex, or national origin. An Equal Employment Opportunity Commission was established to monitor compliance by industries or unions involved in interstate commerce that employed more than twenty-five workers.

The impact of this law, which received the bipartisan support of more than two-thirds of the members of both the House and Senate, was profound. For, according to political observer Theodore H. White,

All the powers of government, prodigious already, were to be invoked to enforce the new measures. Any program, any activity, any institution, any contractor benefiting in any way, small or large, from Federal funds would find those funds cut off if discrimination against anyone could be proved. Universities and hospitals, hotels and theaters, airlines and mail-order houses, unions and manufacturers, cities and states could now be summoned to account for their behavior.

The purpose of the law was, then, to ensure equality; preferential treatment to any individual or to any group on account of perceived imbalances, "which may exist with respect to the total number or percentage of persons of any race, color, religion, sex, or national origin employed by any employer," was expressly prohibited.

Other major legislative accomplishments in 1964 included the Urban Mass Transportation Act, also signed into law in July, and the Wilderness Preservation Act ratified in September. The Transportation Act provided $375 million in Federal grants over a three-year period for the construction and rehabilitation of commuter bus, subway, and train facilities and was the nation's first program of its kind to give massive aid to urban transportation systems. The Wilderness Act set aside 9.1 million acres of forest and mountain preserves, adding some protective barrier around the last of America's fast-disappearing wilderness.

Moving beyond the New Frontier reforms of the Kennedy administration, Johnson set out to stamp his own imprint of reform on the American people. Essentially, the former poor boy from West Texas declared unconditional war on human poverty and unemployment in the United States. The outcome of this offensive, he hoped, would be a Great Society, "a place where the city of man serves not only the needs of the body and the demands of commerce but the desire for beauty and the hunger for community." Johnson seemed deeply troubled by the existence of poverty in the midst of plenty, "the invisible poor" located in Michael Harrington's influential 1962 study, *The Other America*. Harrington estimated that as many as 35 million Americans lived in poverty—too poor even to publicize their plight. Johnson took up the challenge.

The embodiment of the Great Society took the form of the Economic Opportunity Act of late August 1964 as well as other related legislation. Together they attacked the presumed root causes of poverty—particularly illiteracy, unemployment, and inadequate public services. Within a short time nearly $1 billion were appropriated for ten separate programs conducted by the Office of Economic Opportunity, (led by Sargent Shriver, former chief of the Peace Corps and John Kennedy's brother-in-law): among these were the Job Corps: Volunteers in Service to America (VISTA), a domestic Peace Corps; Upward Bound, a program to send underprivileged children to college; Project Head Start, a program for preschool children; work-training and work-study programs; and incentives to small businesses. Other equally ambitious legislation would have to await the outcome of the 1964 presidential election.

The 1964 Presidential Election

The Republican National Convention, meeting in San Francisco in July, nominated Barry M. Goldwater on the first ballot. A senator from Arizona and the champion of a new American conservatism, Goldwater was born in the territory of Arizona three years before its statehood. Of mixed ancestry and son of a devout Episcopalian mother, he became a strong opponent of "Big Government," challenging both the Great Society as well as what he called the "dime store New Deal" of the Eisenhower Administration. His message was simple, and it appealed to the many Americans who had imagined the passing of a simpler life: the danger to freedom, according to his campaign biography *Conscience of a Conservative,* came from the intervention of the Federal government into the lives of individuals, from the graduated income tax to the Social Security system, both of which he saw as unnecessary intrusions into the private sector. The senator also favored militant anticommunism abroad and a tougher stand in Vietnam.

Congressman William E. Miller of New York was chosen as his running mate. Their principal target was Lyndon Johnson, whom Goldwater indicted as, "the biggest [civil rights] faker in the United States," and the "phoniest individual who ever came round." The Goldwater-Miller theme was, "Extremism in the defense of liberty is no vice. Moderation in the pursuit of justice is no virtue." The Republican Conservatives finally got their way.

Meeting in August in Atlantic City, the Democratic National Convention nominated Johnson for a term of his own; the president then smashed tradition by stepping before the delegation to name Senator Hubert H. Humphrey of Minnesota as his personal choice for running mate. Against the lurid image of a demagogic Goldwater with his finger on the "Bomb," all Johnson had to do was look normal. The major polls, Gallup and Harris, predicted a landslide result for the Texan and the effervescent Humphrey. They were right, as the Texan and the "Happy Warrior" from Minneapolis-St. Paul were elected by a landslide with 486 to 52 electoral votes and 43 to 27 million popular votes (61.1 to 38.5 percent, respectively). The Democrats were further strengthened in Congress with a gain of thirty-eight seats in the House and two in the Senate. The GOP, wracked and ruined by the reactionary right of the party, would require the next four years to rethink its strategy.

Toward the Great Society

"We are only at the beginning of the road to the Great Society," declared President Johnson in his January 1965 message to Congress on the State of the Union. "The Great Society," he continued, "asks not how much, but how good; not only how to create wealth but how to use it; not only how fast we are going, but where we are headed."

To prove his point, Johnson and his following in the 89th Congress pushed through the most significant legislation since the days of Franklin Roosevelt. The Elementary and Secondary School Act provided $1.3 billion in aid to public schools under a formula designed to aid the neediest; in addition, it provided $100 million to purchase textbooks and library materials for both public and parochial school children—the first time Federal funds had been authorized to assist nonpublic schools even indirectly. Medicare, a Federal program of health insurance for the elderly under Social Security (first proposed by President Truman in 1945), was passed, as was Medicaid, subsidized medical care for the poor. (Ironically, in 1985 elderly Americans still spent the same proportion—15 percent—of their income on health care costs.) The Voting Rights Act of 1965 struck down literacy and other such tests used in the South to deny blacks the vote, and allowed Federal examiners to register all eligible voters. The Omnibus Housing Act, costing $7.5 billion, was directed toward rent subsidies for low-income families and aid to small businesses displaced by urban renewal. The Clean Air Act amendments required all 1968 and later automobiles to meet Federal control standards. Subsequent years of the Johnson administration witnessed a Model Cities program aimed at encouraging the rehabilitation of city slums; the creation of the Department of Transportation, and legislation creating a nonprofit public corporation (Public Broadcasting Corporation) to accelerate the growth and improve the quality of noncommercial television.

The Great Society attempted to reorient American behavior. An "affirmative action" policy emerged in the form of an executive order in 1965 requiring Federal contractors and institutions to give a better deal to women and nonwhites in employment opportunities. The Truth-in-Lending Act of 1968 required full disclosure to consumers of information related to credit transactions. The newly established National Foundation for the Arts and Humanities financially assisted painters and performing artists, and a revision of the immigration laws, repealing racial quotas that Congress had set in the 1920s, rounded out the legislative landscape of the Great Society.

Expansive and broad-minded, the reforms embodied in the Great Society reflected the dreams, aspirations, and financial priorities of Lyndon Johnson himself, a domestic reformer of the highest order. Like other reformers before him, Johnson would shortly have to decide between guns and butter; experience proved beyond any doubt that no one could have both, not even the president of the United States of America.

The Arrogance of Power

President Johnson had been in office only six months when he was confronted with his first foreign policy crisis—relations with the Republic of Panama. The immediate cause was some student nonsense over rival flags at a high school inside the Canal Zone; before long it turned into dangerous nonsense, indeed, culminating with an attempted invasion of the Zone by a Panamanian mob in January 1964. The mob was finally repulsed by American troops but not before the deaths of three American nationals and an unknown number of Panamanians in the commotion. By April diplomatic relations, which had been broken off by Panama, were restored. More than anything else, the incident demonstrated the extent to which the Panamanians were determined to renegotiate a new Canal Zone treaty with Washington, preferably one that would oversee the passing of American sovereignty and special privileges on Panamanian soil.

Johnson's handling of the Panama crisis was, on balance, considerate and tactful and was well-received in Latin America. Quite different was the reception of his intervention in the Dominican Republic in the spring of 1965. Here, according to most observers, he overreacted to a danger that was partially imaginary. To preserve the position of a military junta of strong anticommunists who opposed the revolt by a group of young officers several days earlier, Johnson announced on April 28, 1965, that he had ordered the landing of United States marines in the Dominican Republic in order to give protection to hundreds of Americans who were presumably in mortal danger. The 556 marines landed at Santo Domingo were soon reinforced by more marines and airborne troops to a total of 21,000. To explain the sending of such a large force, the administration said that the revolutionary movement, originally democratic in purpose, had fallen under the control of communists trained in Cuba and elsewhere, and that intervention alone could prevent turning the Dominican Republic into another Cuba. What was clear was that the American intervention posed a direct violation of the charter of the Organization of American States, despite the subsequent, nominal participation of several other Latin American countries. Right or wrong, the Dominican intervention did bring comparative peace to the island, which witnessed the departure of the last of the so-called Peace Force in September 1966. By then, some troublesome events halfway around the world had begun to consume the energy of the Johnson cabinet.

The overthrow and death of South Vietnam's President Diem was followed in less than three weeks by the assassination of President Kennedy. President Johnson wasted no time in reaffirming the policy objectives of his predecessor regarding Vietnam and called upon all government agencies to support that policy with full unity of purpose. The stability and efficiency that had been hoped for from the new government of military officers did not materialize; in fact, military coups followed one another at frequent intervals until June 1965 when General Nguyen Van Thieu emerged as chief of state with Air Vice-Marshal Nguyen Cao Key as premier.

During the year and a half after Diem's fall, however, the war went badly for Saigon, and LBJ found it necessary to commit major American forces to the area, a decision made in stages, each of which was usually triggered by an allegedly provocative act by the enemy. The first such episode was an attack by North Vietnamese PT-boats on American destroyers cruising international waters in the Gulf of Tonkin during August 1964. Washington retaliated by bombing North Vietnamese naval stations, and Congress, at the president's request, passed a joint resolution authorizing the president "to take all necessary steps to repel any armed attack against the forces of the United States" or "to assist any member or protocol state [of the SEATO treaty] requesting assistance in defense of its freedom." Dubbed the Tonkin Gulf Resolution, it passed the House of Representatives unanimously and the Senate by a vote of 92–2; Johnson and Secretary of State Dean Rusk, the principal official defender of the war, regarded the resolution as "a functional equivalent of a declaration of war," giving the chief executive full authority to escalate the war in any way he saw fit.

By early 1965 there were some twenty-three thousand American troops serving as advisers and only incidentally exposed to the risk of combat in South Vietnam. Attacks by the Viet Cong on American barracks in February altered the picture completely, with American retaliation for specific hostile acts transforming itself into a regular bombing campaign against North Vietnamese military targets. The air war, with all its risks, was carried to within ten miles of the Chinese border. The landing of two Marine battalions at Danang on May 6, 1965, marked the introduction of the first American troops actually deployed for combat in Vietnam; it also marked the Americanization of the war with mostly young American soldiers—average age, nineteen— taking over an increasingly heavy share of fighting on the ground. From there the numbers grew: 180,000 by the end of 1965, 380,000 a year later, 542,000 in 1969. And so, too did the casualties: 350,000 with approximately 56,000 killed (40,000 in combat) by 1973.

American involvement in Vietnam not only became a major American war—and one without a formal declaration of war by the Congress to boot— but also probably the most unpopular episode in the history of United States foreign policy. The loss in national treasure and blood was staggering. According to Pentagon estimates, from 1961 until the final collapse of the Thieu regime in 1975, United States expenditures in Vietnam amounted to a total in excess of $141 billion or, put another way, $7,000 for each of South Vietnam's 20 million people. The war, which was televised daily and which made household words of napalm and free-fire zones, produced a number of dubious precedents, including bombing tonnage (more than three times the tonnage dropped in World War II) and the first-known use of weather warfare.

At home as well as on the battlefield the Vietnam imbroglio took its toll. The economy was undermined by severe inflation beginning in 1965 when the Johnson administration underestimated the war's costs for the coming fiscal year by $10 billion. University campuses were politicized by draft-deferred students. A generation of unpardoned draft resisters fled to Canada and other foreign parts. International confidence in the United States eroded badly. The traditional security of the office of the president was shaken to its very roots.

For his part, LBJ argued that the defense of Vietnam was essential to the containment of Chinese communism, a test of Peking's theory of the inevitable success of communist guerilla warfare. It was also the test case of American determination to hold the line against further communist incursions. "It became increasingly clear," observed the president subsequently in his memoirs, "that Ho Chi Minh's military campaign against South Vietnam was part of a larger, much more ambitious strategy being conducted by the Communists. What we saw taking shape rapidly was a Djakarta-Hanoi-Peking-Pyongyang axis, with Cambodia probably to be brought in as junior partners and Laos to be merely absorbed by the North Vietnamese and Chinese." Given the presumed correctness of these assumptions, concluded the Texan who more than once likened Vietnam to the defense of the Alamo, "The members of this new axis were undoubtedly counting on South Vietnam's collapse and an ignominious American withdrawal."

Americans who argued for continuation of the war or, as some of them did, for waging it more relentlessly were called "hawks"; in August 1965 the Gallup poll indicated that six out of ten Americans approved of United States involvement there. Those who opposed the war were called "doves." These included Senator J. William Fulbright from Arkansas, the Democratic chairman of the Senate Foreign Relations Committee, who had sponsored the original Gulf of Tonkin Resolution; Senator Mike Mansfield (Democrat, Montana), Senate majority leader; and veteran journalist Walter Lippmann, who thought it was a mistake to ask the armed forces to do what was not possible for them to do: i.e., to fight armed peasants who were willing to die. Others opposed the war on the grounds that the United States had no legal obligation under SEATO to defend a regime that was in any case unpopular and repressive.

The war outraged the world. It divided the American people and wasted American resources, starving the Great Society. A victory by North Vietnam, the doves conceded, might make all Vietnam communist, but, clearly, a communist Vietnam, with its ancient hatred and fear of China, would never be a puppet of Peking.

The debate went on, in Congress and in the country, public dissent expanding rapidly from university campuses in 1965 to massive demonstrations and antiwar marches of tens of thousands in 1967 in New York, San Francisco, and Washington, D.C. The longer the war dragged on with no end in sight, the stronger grew the appeal of the doves to an already disillusioned public.

By 1968 the Vietnam War had reached a stalemate. The Viet Cong and North Vietnamese troops could not force the Americans out or destroy the Saigon government; United States troops and their allies, on the other side, could not destroy the Viet Cong or, despite heavy bombing, prevent North Vietnamese supplies and reinforcements from reaching the battle area via the Ho Chi Minh Trail through Laos or through Cambodia. Nor could the Americans prevent attacks on South Vietnamese cities either by rocket-borne bombs or by occasional infiltration.

The most significant illustration of the apparent vulnerability of the government-held area of South Vietnam was the Tet (Lunar New Year) offensive of January-February 1968. Notwithstanding high-level assessments in November 1967 that the United States was winning a war of attrition and that American forces could begin the process of withdrawal within two years, the Viet Cong stunned American public opinion with simultaneous surprise attacks on as many as forty provincial capitals, as well as on a number of American-Vietnamese airfields and bases in the early morning of January 31,1968. The most dramatic episodes were the seizure and six-hour occupation of the American Embassy compound in Saigon by a suicidal Viet Cong unit, and the capture of the capital of Hue by North Vietnamese regulars, from which the invaders were driven out only after weeks of fighting. The Viet Cong took advantage of the occupation of Hue, furthermore, to murder an estimated three thousand supporters of the Saigon regime.

The Viet Cong and their allies were eventually expelled from all the towns and cities that they had siezed, and President Johnson proclaimed the Tet offensive a complete failure, which in military terms it surely was. From the standpoint of Washington, according to Walt Rostow, special assistant to President Johnson, "The surprise was not the scale of the Viet Cong forces revealed but the bold imprudence of the effort: an unlikely diffusion of resources that resulted in a disaster from which the Viet Cong (and their political cadres) never recovered." Still, from this time forward, talk of victory in the war largely ceased.

In addition to producing widespread dissillusionment with the war in general, the Tet offensive accelerated opposition to the president's war policy within the Democratic party itself. In March Senator Eugene McCarthy of Minnesota, running on an antiwar platform, won 42 percent of the vote in the New Hampshire Democratic presidential primary; shortly afterward, Senator Robert F. Kennedy of New York, JFK's brother and a most formidable war critic, entered the presidential race.

Meanwhile, a new consensus was emerging within the administration. Led by the new secretary of defense, Clarke M. Clifford, who succeeded McNamara on March 1, 1968, arguments prevailed that it was useless to press for military victory in Vietnam and that the bombing should be halted as a step toward a negotiated peace.

Accordingly, in a television address on the night of March 31, 1968, President Johnson announced that the bombing would be ended the following day over all of North Vietnam except the sparsely populated southern portion which contained the access routes to South Vietnam. In the same address, and with no hint in the air, the president announced that he would not seek or accept his party's renomination for the presidency.

To the surprise of many, Hanoi responded positively to the president's overture to negotiate. After weeks of wrangling about a place for the talks, both sides accepted Paris, and there on May 10, 1968, delegations headed by veteran diplomats Averell Harriman for the United States and Xuan Thuy for North Vietnam met at last. The results were disappointing, for now Hanoi refused to discuss terms of settlement until all bombing of the North was stopped. This was done on October 31, five days before the presidential election.

Meanwhile, the arms control movement failed to move much beyond the 1963 agreements during the remainder of the 1960s, though Moscow and

Washington managed to agree in January 1967 to internationalizing and de-nuclearizing the use of outer space, the moon, and other celestial bodies. The only other proposal with impact comparable to that of the Partial Nuclear Test Ban Treaty of 1963 was the Nuclear Nonproliferation Treaty, signed in July 1967, which prohibited nuclear states from transferring nuclear weapons or control of such weapons to nonnuclear states and, correlatively, nonnuclear states from manufacturing or otherwise acquiring nuclear weapons and from receiving assistance in the manufacturing of nuclear weapons. Thus, the superpowers saw it to their advantage, if only in a negative way, to preserve the relatively simple but familiar nuclear balance. The treaty's significance was, however, diminished by the refusal of France, China, and India to sign. Further progress was prevented by the Soviet invasion of Czechoslovakia in August 1968 and American involvement in Vietnam.

Urban Racial Violence

Within less than a week of the signing into law of the Voting Rights Act of 1965, the first of the major ghetto riots of the 1960s broke out in the Watts section of Los Angeles, an abject slum and home to a sixth of that city's 523,000 blacks. On August 11, a hot and unusually muggy night in the city, a routine traffic arrest in Watts turned into a riot, with rioters spreading out into the surrounding area, breaking windows, looting stores, and going on a rampage. For the next several days the rioting continued throughout the entire 154 blocks of Watts, as well as in other areas of the city. Not until the fifth day of rioting did authorities, spearheaded by 15,000 National Guard troops, gain the upper hand; by then losses from fires and looting had run into hundreds of millions of dollars. Thousands had been arrested and injured while 28 black lives were lost. Similar violence spread across the country, to Chicago, Illinois, and Springfield, Massachusetts. In the former, a street corner civil rights rally turned into a two-day battle with blacks, the worst outbreak of racial violence in Chicago in over a decade. In the latter, rioting erupted after police arrested civil rights demonstrators blocking the steps of City Hall.

In July 1966 street rioting broke out again on Chicago's largely black West Side, ostensibly over the police decision to turn off fire hydrant water that blacks were using; and again National Guard units were summoned to restore order. In this instance two blacks were killed and six policemen wounded by snipers. The situation eased somewhat the next month when Dr. Martin Luther King, Jr., chairman of the Southern Christian Leadership

Conference, who had challenged Alabama to put an end to racial discrimination in the famous march from Selma to Montgomery in March 1965, announced an agreement with civic leaders and real estate interests in a program to end discrimination in residential renting and sales, paving the way for the Federal Open Housing Law of 1968. But the worst was yet to come. The summer of 1967 brought with it racial rioting in, among other places, Detroit, Michigan, East Harlem, New York, and Newark, New Jersey. Death and destruction lay in the wake of the riots.

The assassination of the thirty-nine-year-old Nobel Prize-winning Dr. King by James Earl Ray on a motel balcony in Memphis on April 4, 1968, set off a week-long wave of urban disturbances in 125 cities encompassing 29 states. Dr. King once quoted an old slave preacher, who said, "We ain't what we ought to be and we ain't what we want to be and we ain't what we're going to be. But thank God we ain't what we was." And because of Martin Luther King's life, the American black was never again the same though the work was far from done.

In the aftermath of the 1967 riots, President Johnson established a National Advisory Commission on Civil Disorders, chaired by Governor Otto Kerner of Illinois. Fourteen hundred pages in length and one-half year in the making, the "Kerner Report," told Americans pretty much what they already knew: "Our nation is moving toward two societies, one black, one white— separate and unequal." Furthermore, the report warned, unless drastic and costly remedies were begun at once, there would be a "continuing polarization of the American community and, ultimately, the destruction of basic democratic values."

Who was to blame for this state of affairs? As far as the commission was concerned, "white racism" lay at the heart of the explosive conditions that ignited riots of the last few summers, civil disorders that were neither caused nor organized by plan or conspiracy. Nonetheless, the report cautioned against a policy of separatism advocated by "Black Power" militants such as Huey Newton's Black Panthers and Stokely Carmichael's increasingly radicalized Student Non-Violent Coordinating Committee, for it could, "only relegate Negroes to a permanently inferior economic state." Among the sweeping recommendations made at the Federal and local levels were changes in law enforcement, welfare, employment, education, and news media.

Though no attempt was made to put a price tag on the panel's recommendations, it was abundantly clear that they went far beyond further proposed legislation of the Great Society. Answering the "guns versus butter" quandary, a *New York Times* editorial expressed a sentiment shared by a majority of the American people in 1968: "The first necessity [for national action on the racial problem] is for a long overdue reordering of priorities in Washington—a turn toward de-escalation of the military combat in Vietnam and escalation of the war against poverty and discrimination at home." The growing migration of rural blacks to urban areas by 1970—16.8 million out of a total black population of 22.5 million—attested to the urgency of the task ahead. At the same time, other Americans set out to reorder their own priorities.

A New Radicalism

In protesting the war in Vietnam, poverty and racism at home, and the traditional patterns of education and employment, a new radicalism in social thought emerged in the 1960s. Though often identified as a revolt of the young, it was, as historian Robert Allen Skotheim has argued, both less and more than that, for while nearly 14 million souls swelled the ranks of the youth population in the 1960s, only a minority of them participated directly in or expressed sympathy for political dissent and the search for a new lifestyle. But as is often the case among intellectuals in relation to the whole society from which they were estranged, the young radicals, whose motto was, "You can't trust anyone over thirty," had an influence out of all proportion to their numbers.

Their favorite philosophers ranged from Herbert Marcuse whose *One Dimensional Man* helped them locate totalitarianism in the government and society of the United States, to Jean Paul Sartre whose *No Exit* said it all; their favorite historians were Barton Bernstein of Stanford University and Howard Zinn of Boston University; their favorite musicians were Joan Baez and Bob Dylan; their favorite films were *The Graduate* and *Easy Rider;* and their favorite highs were marijuana and LSD (lysergic acid diethylamide).

The New Radicalism or New Left, as it was sometimes called, was a pluralistic, amorphous grouping, embracing among others the Free Speech Movement, the Students for a Democratic Society, and the various antiwar organizations composed mainly of white, middle-class youth. Furthermore, the New Radicalism, according to one close student of the subject, Jack Newfield, operated essentially on three levels. On the political level, it was an anti-Establishment protest against all the obvious inequities of American life; on a more complex level, it was a moral revulsion against society that was perceived as being increasingly corrupt; and on the last level, it was an existential revolt against remote, impersonal forces that were not responsive to human needs. For some, solutions to those problems required figuratively reaching out and grabbing their university administrations by the throat, forcing the termination of such practices as armed forces recruitment and the curtailment of Pentagon-related research on campus, or the introduction of a more "relevant" curriculum. The result was turmoil and violence at universities from California to New York, culminating with the shooting to death of four students on the campus of Kent State University by National Guardsmen in May 1970.

By the end of the decade, "The Movement" was gone, the victim of its own infighting. More and more, its most extreme exponents turned further and further in a leftward direction, appealing to violence and losing touch with the dreams and aspirations of their natural constituencies. Others became insurance salesmen and stockbrokers. In the end, the New Radicalism could not justify the political supremacy of a minority of intellectuals who could not even shape their own academic institutions, much less persuade the majority of Americans that the culture in which they lived was a form of fascism.

Not to be outdone, Hispanics, American Indians, and women all created their own liberation movement, each hoping, in its own way, to throw "the man" off their back. Hispanics, or Spanish-speaking Americans, numbered nearly 20 million, making the United States the fourth-largest Spanish-speaking nation in the world. Destined to outnumber blacks by the end of the 1980s, Hispanics came from such places as Cuba, Puerto Rico, and, of course, Mexico. Almost eight hundred thousand Puerto Ricans alone lived in New York, accounting for one-third of that city's welfare recipients. Six million Mexican-Americans, resident largely in the Southwest, suffered unemployment at twice the national level. Many eked out an existence as migrant laborers in California's "farm factories." Their leaders, including César Chávez whose National Farm Workers association championed the migrants' cause, adopted the term *Chicano* to describe their cultural identity. They demanded bilingual instruction in the public schools and sought legal remedy to rectify perceived past injustices in the workplace and marketplace. They were only partially successful.

Well outside the mainstream of national life were the American Indians. Though their population grew at four times the national rate in the 1960s, reaching nearly eight hundred thousand in 1970, their prospects were dim: their unemployment was the highest in the nation, as was their infant mortality, alcoholism, and suicide rates; the only thing less than average was life expectancy—forty-six years compared with the national average of sixty-nine. Worse yet, the Department of the Interior's Bureau of Indian Affairs had done little to alleviate horrendous conditions on Federal reservations. In protest to these and other grievances, particularly claims to recover ancestral land, the American Indian Movement (A.I.M.) was formed, drawing attention to its people's conditions by temporarily occupying public places linked to their vanishing past. Some actions were peaceful; others were violent. All had little impact. More successful was the women's liberation movement of the 1960s.

The Women's Liberation Movement

There were at least three strains or groups of women who merged in the late 1960s to become known as the women's liberation movement: the group of mature, professional women such as sociologist Alice Rossi and Democratic Congresswoman Martha Griffiths of Michigan, who had been working behind the scenes in the late 1950s for legislation benefiting women (favorable clauses in the Social Security Act as well as antidiscriminatory legislation in general); the college-educated white, middle-class housewives who lived in the suburbs at the opening of the decade and who responded dramatically to Betty Friedan's *Feminine Mystique* published in 1963; and the new generation of college-age women who represented the largest single group of women ever to gain higher education. Many in this latter group worked in the civil rights movement at the beginning of the decade and the anti-Vietnam movement in the middle of the decade. It was after 1967 that they moved on to form the radical wing of the women's movement.

These three, distinct groups came together at the end of the decade because they recognized that they shared more complaints than they had ever imagined, principally that the "oppression of women" was universal and not restricted to one class or race, and that expressive politics—demonstrations, rallies, and confrontations—that had characterized all of the other social movements of the decade could well be applied to women's issues.

Their leaders were drawn from all three groups: Betty Friedan became the spokeswoman for the frustrated suburban housewife; Alice Rossi, Esther Peterson, and Martha Griffiths became the representatives of the professional woman; and Shulamith Firestone, Robin Morgan, and Kate Millett became key speakers for the militant women's liberationist. Gloria Steinem and Jane Fonda, attractive celebrities with reputations established in other areas outside women's liberation, also became speakers for women's issues.

The speeches and writings of these and many other women were widely circulated and received a great deal of headline and front-page coverage by the end of the decade and into the early 1970s. They all generally agreed that women had been segregated into the lowest-paying jobs in the marketplace; that many had been consigned to the role of domestic servant and baby machine; and that neither universities, businesses, nor the government took women seriously as equal human beings with the same rights and opportunities as men.

They differed, however, in their methods and ultimate goals for the women's movement. While the radicals preached separatism and lesbianism, the liberal middle advocated legislative remedies, scrupulous advocacy of equal opportunity laws, and the improvement of man-woman relations. Some women in the movement identified with the "equal pay-equal work" slogan; others insisted on equal admission of women into professional schools; still others experimented with new marriage relationships in which men shared the homemaking and child-rearing tasks with women and in which they shared paid employment (either both part-time or alternating full-time work).

Still others insisted that men and women could never live harmoniously in Western, capitalistic culture. Some radical feminists shared the Marxist critique of Western society and, though they were often hard-pressed to find a desirable alternative in the socialist world, they envisioned a more ideal future. Some feminists espoused Maoism in the 1960s and defended Mao's versions of the egalitarian society until the drastic consequences of the Cultural Revolution made this claim impossible to hold any longer.

The climate within which the women's movement thrived after 1967 was one in which a wide variety of social reforms were promulgated. Feminism has always had the most success in times when other social reforms have been proposed (the Progressive period is the closest example; the abolitionist period the more distant example). Criticism of American foreign policy in Vietnam, the well-organized protests of the civil rights movement, the critique of higher education, and the ecology movement that was getting underway, all provided a sympathetic environment for a discussion and examination of woman's role in American life. After all, women were the numerical majority in the country, yet they seemed more deprived culturally and legally than any minority whose rights were being vigorously espoused.

Even before these three groups merged into an uneasy coalition at the end of the decade (and the coalition did not last beyond the mid-1970s), there was evidence in the national administration of concern over women's issues. At the beginning of the decade, President Kennedy appointed a number of prominent women, including Eleanor Roosevelt and Esther Peterson (assistant secretary of labor), to the Commission on the Status of Women. This illustrious commission investigated the working conditions of women in government, industry, and education as well as the prevailing laws regarding women's opportunities in higher education, and it prepared a major report called "American Women" that was published in 1963. In particular, the report called attention to the fact that one of the worst discriminators against women was the Federal government, and JFK called for all Federal agencies to examine their practices and procedures and eliminate all discriminatory forms.

In 1963, Congress passed the Equal Pay Act sponsored by Representative Edith Green (Democrat, Oregon), a fighter for women's rights for many years. Indeed, the few women in the House of Representatives joined by the few in the Senate (particularly Maurine Neuberger, Democrat, Oregon) worked against great odds in the late 1950s and early 1960s to secure legislation favorable to women. The word *sex* was introduced into the Civil Rights Law of 1964, and Congress thereby forbade discrimination in employment on the basis of gender as well as race and religion. Through the offices of the Equal Employment Opportunities Commission, women sought legal remedies more and more. The publicity that accompanied the Civil Rights Law and the coupling of civil rights for black Americans with all women served to educate Americans on the common needs of both groups and, indeed, one of the greatest accomplishments of the women's movement in the 1960s was acquainting everyone with the issues of feminism. Women educated themselves in new groups called "consciousness raising sessions" where they discussed their experiences and examined them for evidences of sexism. The American vocabulary was enlarged by feminism: words such as *sexism* and *male chauvinism* were introduced into common usage. Though hostility to men was not characteristic of the movement as a whole, most feminists were not averse to labeling particular men who exhibited sexist attitudes toward women as *male chauvinists*. The goal was for men also to do some soul-searching and consciousness raising, and many did.

Another social movement that became very popular toward the end of the decade contributed in no small measure to the mood and ethos of the women's movement; this was the mental health movement. Part of the general reexamination of American society that so invigorated many young Americans in the 1960s was the effort to democratize the psychiatric profession. Group therapy became common and flourished in this period and beyond. "Consciousness raising" sessions shared many characteristics with group therapy sessions. Both sought to examine the individual's life history, wth the support and help of the group (and sometimes the professional aid of the leader), and to give advice for short-term problems. The assumption underlying this process of self- and group-education was a very American assumption: knowledge will set you free. Before women could go into places of power where they had never trod before—before women could assert themselves with their husbands and auto mechanics—they had to understand how their diffidence, their self-image, and their adult roles had come to be. Before they could challenge the male establishment, they had to develop the self-confidence that was essential to a successful confrontation. Thus assertiveness training courses for women became extremely popular too.

Typical of one of the most exciting reform periods of American history, the 1960s and the women's liberation movement existed in a time when education, legislation, judicial change, occupational changes all occurred simultaneously. The 1960s witnessed the coming of age of the first group of Baby Boomers. Colleges burst at the seams, welcoming larger and larger numbers of students for the first time in American history. The economy, until the end of the decade when Vietnam soured it, was prospering with minimal levels of inflation. The mood was one of frustration and optimism, mixed uneasily together. But, with change, the phenomenon of rising expectations also developed. As Congress responded to black American demands, their demands increased; as students protested the draft, the war heated up. As women began organizing in their own behalf, they kept expanding their goals. The 1970s would see many of the issues raised in the 1960s persist as vital concerns. There would be a reexamination and reassessment of many issues as well. But the enthusiasm, the demonstrations, and the coalescing of various social reform movements remained unique to the 1960s. Television played a major role in publicizing the issues and the personalities of the movements in the sixties in an unprecedented way. No war would ever again not be a TV war; no demonstration would go unnoticed. Though coalitions formed in the 1960s were destined to disintegrate in the 1970s for lack of a common focus, many of the leaders and articulators of the key women's issues would remain for years to come as leaders in the movement.

The Reincarnation of "Mr. Republican"

The Republican National Convention, gathering in Miami in early August 1968, nominated former Vice-President Richard M. Nixon for the presidency on the first ballot. Since his razor-thin loss to JFK in 1960, and more substantial loss to Democrat Pat Brown for the governorship of California in

1962, Nixon moved to New York City where he practiced law until 1968. In the years since the Goldwater debacle, he proved himself the politician's politician, cultivating Republicans at the grassroots level. The favorite of party professionals, big contributors, and the rank-and-file who controlled the party machinery in the conservative Middle West and South, Nixon easily pushed aside the challenges of Governor Nelson Rockefeller of New York and Governor George Romney of Michigan. "The time has come for us to leave the valley of despair and climb the mountain so that we may see the glory of the dawn of a new day for America, a new dawn for peace and freedom to the world," declared the Republican presidential nominee in his acceptance speech. Promising an end to "the long dark night for America," Nixon proclaimed that, on the foreign front, he would make the end of the war in Vietnam his first order of business; on the domestic front, he would solve the nation's internal problems by combining a firm approach to law and order with innovative remedies to poverty that would depend less on Federal aid and more on private enterprise. Specifics were kept purposely vague. As his running mate, Nixon chose Governor Spiro Agnew of Maryland, a conservative public administrator and the son of a Greek immigrant and restaurant owner in Baltimore.

The Democratic National Convention, meeting in Chicago in late August, nominated Vice-President Humphrey for the presidency. Humphrey was the beneficiary of a series of events that would otherwise have made his nomination problematical: President Johnson's decision to withdraw from politics, the assassination of challenger Senator Robert F. Kennedy in June, and the inability of Senator Eugene J. McCarthy to sustain the momentum of his unexpected success in the New Hampshire primaries. Humphrey was clearly the choice of labor unions, city machines, black organizations, and farm groups. He had also managed the difficult task of mollifying southern conservatives without alienating northern liberals. His hand-picked vice-presidential running mate was Senator Edmund S. Muskie of Maine, the son of a Polish immigrant. Confident and assured in his own way that he could find a way out of the Vietnam war, Humphrey had all but lost touch with the young antiwar protestors whose presence in Chicago led to violent street clashes with the local police within a few blocks of the convention's center and within full view of the American TV public.

Inside, the Democratic Convention delegates appeared as bitterly divided on the issue of Vietnam as the protestors and the police in the street. Ugly scenes, name calling and nastiness, in both places, were there for all to see. The nomination of segregationist Governor George C. Wallace of Alabama and Vietnam-hardliner General Curtis E. LeMay as presidential and vice-presidential candidates of the American Independent party, with the real threat of throwing the election into the United States House of Representatives, rounded off the principals in an already extraordinary presidential campaign. As the election neared, the major public opinion polls predicted a very close outcome, and they were right.

Nixon, bringing to a climax one of the most amazing personal comebacks in American poltical history, edged out Humphrey in a close and tumultuous presidential campaign. In the popular vote column, victory held the barest of margins: 31,785,480 votes (43.4 percnt) to 31,275,166 (42.7 percent) or, put differently, only four-tenths of a percentage point. In the electoral column, a different story emerged with 302 electoral votes to 191, with one elector voting for Wallace. Joining the ranks of Thomas Jefferson and Andrew Jackson, Nixon became only the third man to be elected to the White House after having been previously defeated for the presidency. And, although many distrusted his personality, even Nixon's most severe critics recognized the president as intelligent and able, essentially a moderate conservative. He would in fact require all of these qualities in dealing with a Democratic-controlled Congress. The 37th president of the United States would be the first president since 1892 whose party controlled neither the House (243–192) nor the Senate (58–42) at the time of his inauguration. In any case, Richard Nixon finally had the job that he desperately wanted and the American people had the change of government they thought they needed. The New Frontier and Great Society now seemed a million light years away.

Suggested Readings

Baskir, Lawrence M. and Strauss, William A. *Chance and Circumstance: The Draft, the War and the Vietnam Generation.* 1978.

Berman, Larry. *Planning a Tragedy: The Americanization of the War in Vietnam.* 1982.

Berman, Ronald. *America in the Sixties.* 1968.

Bornet, Vaughn D. *The Presidency of Lyndon B. Johnson.* 1984.

Dugger, Ronnie. *The Politican: The Life and Times of Lyndon Johnson.* 1982.

Fulbright, J. William. *The Arrogance of Power.* 1966.

––––––– . *The Crippled Giant.* 1972.

Halberstam, David. *The Best and the Brightest.* 1972.

Harrington, Michael. *The Other American.* 1962.

Heath, Jim F. *Decade of Disillusionment.* 1974.

Herring, George. *America's Longest War.* 1979.

Johnson, Lyndon B. *The Vantage Point*. 1976.

Kearns, Doris. *Lyndon Johnson and the American Dream*. 1976.

Lerner, Gerda, ed. *The Female Experience*. 1977.

Newfield, Jack. *A Prophetic Minority*. 1966.

Podhoretz, Norman. *Why We Were in Vietnam*. 1982.

Polenberg, Richard. *One Nation Divisible: Class, Race and Ethnicity in the U.S. Since 1938*. 1980.

Skotheim, Robert Allen. *Totalitarianism and American Social Thought*. 1971.

Sochen, June. *Movers and Shakers: American Women Thinkers and Activists, 1900–1970*. 1973.

————. *Herstory: A Women's View of American History*. (2d ed.). 1981.

Taggart, Robert. *The Promise of Greatness*. 1976.

Unger, Irwin. *The Movement*. 1974.

White, Theodore H. *America in Search of Itself*. 1982.

5

The Beleaguered Presidency: The Nixon Years

"We cannot learn from one another," declared Richard Nixon uncharacteristically in his inaugural address of January 20, 1969, "until we stop shouting at one another—until we speak quietly enough so that our words can be heard as well as our voices." Eschewing the hawkish, political, and combative Nixon of the past, President Nixon was prepared to listen and "to listen in new ways—to the voices of anguish, the voices that speak without words, the voices of the heart, to the injured voices, the anxious voices, the voices that have despaired of being heard." For those who had been left out of participating in the American Dream, he would try to bring them in; for those who had been left behind, he would help them to catch up. In an apparent reference to winding down the Vietnam war, the president observed that, "We shall plan now for the day when our wealth can be transferred from the destruction of war abroad to the urgent needs of our people at home," though it was equally clear that he foresaw that there were limits to what government alone could do. To the Soviet Union, Nixon offered peaceful competition instead of conflict. The times were, he supposed, on the side of peace.

Not surprisingly perhaps, hawkish Republicans felt betrayed by the emergence of this new Nixon; many opposition Democrats remained cynical. Was it really possible for this self-acknowledged political man, this genius of political opportunism, to avoid the temptation of extremism? Had he not gone out of his way to praise the Democrats, enlist youth, and reach out to the blacks? "I know America," he said. "I know the heart of America is good."

President Nixon surrounded himself with competent if undramatic personalities. For his secretary of state he chose William P. Rogers, a lawyer who had served as attorney general in the Eisenhower administration; for secretary of defense, Congressman Melvin R. Laird of Wisconsin, a member of the House Armed Services Committee and a strong supporter of the war in Vietnam; and as attorney general, John N. Mitchell, presidential campaign manager and the president's New York law firm associate.

Despite his poor image among the nation's intellectuals, the president was able to attract two distinguished members of the Harvard University faculty into his administration: Daniel P. Moynihan and Henry A. Kissinger. Flamboyant and innovative, Moynihan sought to assist Nixon in transforming the nation's welfare into a new work-rewarding system whereby, instead of Federal welfare grants, the government would make a cash grant to guarantee a minimum income level; the proposal and its controversial provisions became known as the Nixon-Moynihan Family Assistance Plan—and managed to alienate so many politicians and constituencies that it was eventually abandoned.

Kissinger, a German Jew who had emigrated to the United States in 1938, was named assistant for national security affairs. Among other things, Kissinger served as the administration's intellectual formulator of détente, a diplomatic strategy designed to manage relations both with the Soviet Union and China. In particular, he sought to engage Moscow in an intricate network of commercial and other relations, with a view to increasing the Kremlin's stake in peace. As part of the carrot-and-stick approach, it was necessary to make clear to the Soviets that there was an iron link between their external behavior and the West's willingness to deal economically with them; in this sense, trade was perceived as a technique for opening the way to other agreements, establishing a continuing process of negotiation, and advancing peaceful change within the Soviet sphere of influence. A brilliant strategy in many respects, détente, as conceived and played out by the administration, would enjoy a number of spectacular if limited successes.

Peace with Honor in Vietnam

While still hoping to end the war through negotiations, which had stalled over conflicting peace proposals, President Nixon attempted to assuage criticism at home by a process of "Vietnamization," i.e., the gradual withdrawal of American forces and their replacement by South Vietnamese troops with improved training and equipment. An annoucement on June 8, 1969, that 25,000 U.S. troops would be withdrawn during July, to be replaced by South Vietnamese, marked the beginning of the end of American involvement. The president's first comprehensive exposition of the new policy came in a television address to the nation on November 3, less than a month after a quarter of a million antiwar protestors descended on Washington. All U.S. combat forces, explained Nixon, reaching out to what he perceived to be "the great silent majority" of his fellow Americans, would be withdrawn and replaced by South Vietnamese on an orderly, scheduled timetable. The timetable, in turn, would depend on the progress of the peace talks, the scale of enemy activity, and progress in the training of South Vietnamese troops. He warned Hanoi, whose leader Ho Chi Minh had died in September, that any increase in violence would be met by strong and effective response—renewed bombing of the North. An announcement in December that 50,000 additional American troops would be withdrawn in April 1970 went a long way toward taking the steam out of the antiwar movement, an effect noted on the nation's uneasy campuses.

Such comparative harmony came to a sudden halt on April 30, 1970, with Nixon's declaration that American and South Vietnamese forces were carrying the war into Cambodia in order to destroy communist bases there. For years areas adjoining South Vietnam had been employed as Viet Cong sanctuaries with the tacit consent of nominally neutralist Prince Norodom Sihanouk, the Cambodian chief of state.

Washington had long tolerated this breach of neutrality rather than taking action that might have otherwise driven the prince into the enemy's camp, but a new situation had arisen with the emergence of a pro-West leadership that found itself threatened by the presence of thousands of North Vietnamese ensconced in the sanctuaries. Faced with this threat, the new Cambodian government of General Lon Nol requested the urgent assistance of the United States and other allies. Going to the presumed "heart of the trouble," President Nixon responded with an intense ground and air attack against the enemy-held sanctuaries, promising to remove the forces no later than June 30.

The thrust into Cambodia looked to many Americans like an expansion of the war, producing yet another round of demonstrations on university campuses. The most violent of the campus protests occurred on May 4 when four unarmed students were killed in a skirmish between Ohio National Guardsmen and antiwar protestors at Kent State University in Kent, Ohio. From the Senate came the introduction of several resolutions designed to prevent the administration from widening hostilities in Indochina without the consent of Congress. Upon completion of the sweep through the sanctuaries on June 30, Nixon issued a report claiming outstanding success for the operation, even though the "key control center" of the communist command had not been located.

In November the administration turned its attention to the large buildup of military supplies in North Vietnam, the problem being one of preventing their movement southward. To meet the challenge, the United States in February 1971 launched what was to be the last major offensive of the war; with American air cover only, the South Vietnamese were provided with their first real test at fighting on the field alone. Though not very successful, it did appear that Vietnamizaion of the war was well underway. Thereafter, until the Paris Ceasefire Agreement was finally signed in January 1973, the administration resorted to increased bombing raids in the North to meet increased fighting in the South and as a means of prodding Hanoi to the peace table.

The last American troops were withdrawn in March 1973, two months after the ceasefire and eight years after the first formal commitment of military forces. Hanoi regarded the agreement as a scrap of paper and completed its goal of reunifying the two Vietnams by force of arms in April 1975. The collapse of Saigon together with the defeat of pro-Western elements in Cambodia (and subsequently Laos) marked the end of American influence in the area, giving some substance to the row of falling dominoes alluded to by Eisenhower in the 1950s.

Even before the collapse of the American position in Southeast Asia, the lessons of Vietnam were presumably being translated into policy at the highest levels. In his report to Congress in 1971, President Nixon noted that there were, "lessons to be learned from our Vietnam experience—about unconventional warfare and the role of outside countries, the nature of commitments [and] the need for public understanding and support." The net result of such thinking was the so-called Nixon Doctrine, the logical corollary to Vietnamization. In the case of nonnuclear aggression, Nixon went on record, "We shall furnish military and economic assistance when requested in accordance with our treaty requirements." Manpower would, however, come from the nation under threat. And though some argued that such a policy in fact raised the nuclear threshold, none could doubt that the president's words accurately reflected the mood of the nation. The *New York Times* publication in June of the so-called Pentagon Papers, a massive study conducted by the Pentagon three years earlier, of how the United States went to war in Indochina, merely reinforced in the American public the belief that the Vietnam War had been wrong. The attempt of Attorney General Mitchell to block the release of further information from this source on the legal ground that it would cause "irreparable injury to the defense interests of the United States"—ultimately rejected by the Supreme Court in *New York Times* v. *United States*—produced further disillusionment with the administration. None could doubt that militarily the United States failed in Vietnam: that the army failed to assess its technical problems, that the White House foolishly left the issue to the army, and that the overall inability to field enough troops and sustain them had lost everything.

On the positive side, the Vietnam debate enlarged and encouraged congressional participation in the foreign policy process, a long-overdue adjustment to the use and abuse of executive power in this field since 1945; and it was precisely this participation that averted a recrudescence of "McCarthyism" and "stab in the back" theories, the latter propagated by no less than former South Vietnamese President Nguyen Van Thieu. Senate Majority Leader Mansfield observed much to his credit at the end of the conflict, "There is not profit at this time in hashing over the might-have-beens of the past. Nor is there any value in finger-pointing." Most Americans concurred.

Arms Control

During his first year in office, Nixon agreed to resume talks with the Soviets and in November 1969 the Strategic Arms Limitation Talks (SALT) began in Helsinki. The task of further arms limitations was complicated by two new technological developments—the antiballistic missile (ABM) and the multiple independently targetable re-entry vehicle (MIRV). The two developments were closely related for one was a counter to the other. The ABM system, which the Soviets began to deploy around Moscow in the late sixties and may in fact have been only an anti-plane net, promised a defense against missile attack, threatening to neutralize the second-strike capability of the United States.

With evidence of potential Soviet ABM deployment, America followed suit. In order to overpower the ABM defense, the United States developed the MIRV missile, able to carry aloft multiple nuclear warheads that could be released in flight to come down separately against one or more targets. The United States proceeded to operationalize the MIRV technology with the Minuteman-III ICBM and the submarine-launched Poseidon C-3 missile. The Minuteman and Poseidon MIRV programs increased by more than fourfold the number of reentry vehicles of the U.S. strategic forces, easily providing the capability of overcoming any possible Soviet ABM system.

As well as countering an ABM system, MIRV technology, which the Soviet Union also began to implement in the mid-seventies, served to increase counterforce capabilities, i.e., the ability to strike directly at the enemy's nuclear forces. This proved a dangerously destabilizing influence, for multiplying the number of warheads made conceivable, for the first time, a preemptive strike by the Soviet Union. Using only a part of its ICBM force in order to destroy almost all of the U.S. land-based ICBMs would still have left the Soviets with substantial force to threaten American cities in the event the United States should retaliate. Such a development highlighted the crucial importance of the submarine arm of the American Triad in insuring a credible, mutually assured destruction (MAD) capability and led to the proposal to develop a mobile land-based system to avoid the presumed vulnerability of the existing ICBMs.

While the dynamics of technology drove the arms race forward, the superpowers pursued a course of arms control in the early seventies. In 1971 the two nations signed not only the Seabed Treaty, in which they agreed not to place nuclear weapons on the seabed or the ocean floor, but also the "Hot Line" Modernization and Nuclear Accidents Agreement to reduce the precipitant or accidental use of nuclear weapons. It was in 1972, however, that the SALT negotiations produced their first results. In May of that year President Nixon and Soviet Party Secretary Leonid Brezhnev signed in Moscow the Anti-Ballistic Missile Treaty, permitting only two ABM sites for each nation (reduced to one in 1974) and the Interim Agreement on Strategic Offensive Arms, which imposed a five-year freeze on the number of fixed ICBMs and SLBM launchers then operational or under construction in each nation. During this freeze the two sides agreed to negotiate a more comprehensive treaty of longer duration to limit offensive weapons. These agreements, known as SALT I, confirmed Nixon's acceptance of the reality of a rough nuclear parity or essential equivalence.

The China Opening

The administration, led by the president and National Security Adviser Kissinger, clearly desired a normalization of relations with China, as indeed did Peking with Washington. Drawn by common interests, both sides recognized the need to block the expansionism of the Soviet Union. Peking understood, observed Nixon in retrospect, that the United States was the only country with the power to blunt the Soviet thrust for hegemony in Asia; on the other hand, the United States understood that, while China was communist, it did not threaten American interests and could well serve as a counterpoise to Moscow. A consensus had been reached all around.

After a vote in the U.N. General Assembly in November 1970 showing a majority in favor of seating the Peking government, the White House ordered a review of American policy toward the communist giant. In his second "State of the World" message to Congress, February 25, 1971, the president broke precedent by referring to the Peking government by its official title, the "People's Republic of China." Other conciliatory moves from Washington included a further relaxation of the ban on American travel to China, itself reciprocated in an unexpected manner when an American table tennis team, competing in Tokyo, was suddenly invited to visit China in early April. Speculation on the significance of "ping pong diplomacy" was heightened when Premier Chou En-lai personally greeted the visiting team, observing that a new page in the relations of the Chinese and American people had opened. And, indeed it had. Determined to take advantage of his historic opportunity and fully prepared to relinquish the fiction that Taiwan was the sole legitimate representative of the mainland Chinese, President Nixon stunned the world by his announcement on July 15, 1971, that he had received and accepted an invitation to visit Peking in 1972. In the United States, the surprising news got a generally favorable reception, except in strongly conservative circles.

Speculation that the proposed American visit to Peking augured well for the almost certain admission of communist China to the United Nations proved accurate; for even while the summit agenda was being fashioned, on October 25, 1971, the General Assembly approved a resolution calling simultaneously for the seating of the People's Republic of China and the expulsion of Taiwan. Accompanied by an army of media personnel, representatives from the State Department, and the ubiquitous Henry Kissinger, Nixon was, for more than one week in February 1972, hosted and toasted by a succession of Chinese dignitaries including Chairman Mao. From a viewing standpoint, it was a television spectacular, replete with the president's walk on the Great Wall of China, which had originally been intended to keep the barbarians at bay.

Atmospherics aside, the actual substance of the talks was contained in the text of the quickly dubbed "Shanghai Communique" released at the conclusion of the final meeting between President Nixon and Premier Chou En-lai. After reaffirming the desirability of continued normalization of relations between their countries, the two leaders acknowledged that Taiwan was an "internal" problem for the Chinese people to work out for themselves, though Nixon expected the final solution to be a peaceful one. With this as a goal the president approved the ultimate objective of the withdrawal of American forces and installations from that island, while in the meantime reducing existing forces as tensions in the area diminished. Finally, the two sides agreed to stay in contact through various channels, including the sending of a senior U.S. representative to Peking from time to time (later established as a liaison mission), for concrete consultation with a view toward complete normalization of relations, i.e., the formal exchange of ambassadors.

A Change in the Wind

Nixon had come to the presidency with the conviction that the Supreme Court of the 1950s and 1960s under the leadership of Chief Justice Earl Warren had become politically active, attempting to use its interpretation of the law to remake American society according to its own lights. Regarding himself as a legal and political moderate conservative, Nixon jumped at the opportunity to replace the seventy-eight-year-old Warren, who had already indicated his intention to retire. After some consideration Nixon finally settled upon Judge Warren E. Burger of the District of Columbia Court of Appeals in his choice for the fifteenth chief justice in the nation's history. An exponent of law and order in society and philosophically a moderate conservative himself, Burger easily won confirmation in the Democratic-controlled Senate in June 1969.

A second opportunity presented itself with the departure, in the same year, of Justice Abe Fortas who resigned after disclosure of alleged shady financial practices. This time the president ran into rough sledding on his first two appointments to the post; two Southerners, Clement Haynsworth, chief judge of the U.S. Court of Appeals in the 4th Circuit, and G. Harrold Carswell, judge of the U.S. Court of Appeals for the 5th Circuit, were rejected by the Senate. Civil rights groups opposed Haynsworth as a racist—a "laundered segregationalist"—while others opposed him as antilabor; Carswell was opposed both as a racist and as a mediocre mind. The president's third nomination, Judge Harry A. Blackmun of the Federal Circuit Court of Appeals and a Northerner, was however unanimously confirmed by the Senate in May 1970.

The strict constructionist character of the Burger Court was strengthened a year later when the death of Justice Black and the resignation of Justice Harlan allowed the administration to place two additional conservatives on the bench: Assistant Attorney General William Rhenquist of Arizona and

Lewis Powell, a Virginia attorney and former president of the American Bar Association. Thus in the space of several years, Richard Nixon had the unique opportunity to change the Supreme Court—though probably not as much as he would have liked.

In the area of civil rights, the administration pursued a policy that was apparently supposed to accommodate as many interest groups as possible. In July 1969, after five months of internal debate, Attorney General Mitchell and Secretary of Health, Education and Welfare (HEW) Robert H. Finch indicated they intended to hold southern school districts—except for those with "bona fide education and administrative problems" such as "serious shortages of necessary physical facilities, financial resources or faculty"—to the September 1969 deadline for desegregation. While far less conciliatory to southern whites than originally expected, the guidelines equally failed to mollify liberal critics who charged that the policy would open the door to more and more delays in the desegregation of southern schools. Then, in August, HEW and the Department of Justice argued in court that HEW-approved desegregation plans should be withdrawn and desegregation delayed. The administration's tactical shift from lawsuits to Federal fund cutoffs prompted the resignation of the chief of the Civil Rights Office at HEW, Leon Panetta, a strong advocate of Federal intervention.

In March 1970, the president announced that he would request $1.5 billion from Congress to improve educational facilities in so-called racially impacted areas as well as to help resolve problems caused by court-directed desegregation. In emphasizing the distinction between *de jure* segregation grounded in discriminatory legislation and *de facto* segregation reflecting residential patterns—a particularly different problem in northern cities—the chief executive promised that transporting children by bus beyond normal geographical school zones would not be employed to redress racial imbalance. And in 1971, as a sop to suburbanites who controlled most legislatures in the urbanized states, the president asserted he would oppose federally forced integration of the suburbs. This assuaged the fears of many such residents as more Americans in metropolitan areas, for the first time in the nation's history, lived outside the city limits rather than within them. Also in 1971 the Voting Rights Act of 1965 was extended to prohibit literacy tests as a qualification for voting in presidential elections and was applied to northern areas where these tests had been required.

Other notable legislation in the first two years of the administration included the National Environment Policy Act of 1969, pledging Washington to a "now or never" fight against pollution; the Water Quality Improvement

Act of 1970 which, among other things, authorized the Federal government to clean up disastrous oil spills; the Postal Reorganization Act which replaced the 181-year-old Post Office Department with an independent government agency; the Clean Air Act of 1970, which set a six-year deadline for the automobile industry to develop an engine that would be nearly free of hydrocarbons, carbon monoxide, and nitrogen oxide; the Legislative Reorganization Act, which provided for public recording of roll-call voters in various congressional committees; and a spate of "law and order" acts spearheaded by the Organized Crime Control Act of 1970, which provided for immunity for witnesses giving testimony, special grand juries to investigate organized crime, and limited disclosure of electronic surveillance.

The most controversial legislation in 1971, together with the elimination of funding for the eighteen hundred mile per hour supersonic transport plane (the SST), was the Draft Extension Act. Consuming more than half the Senate's time that year, the act provided for a two-year extension of the president's draft authority (to June 30, 1973), an end to student deferments, and no significant limit on the president's conduct of the war in Vietnam or his policy. The increase of total pay and allowances for servicemen of $2.4 billion annually was designed principally to induce enough men to volunteer for the military so that the draft would not be required by the time the new law expired; in its place would stand an all-volunteer force, subsequently achieved.

Nixon, who had come to the presidency in the belief that the American economy operated best with the least governmental interference, soon found that traditional Republican orthodoxy could do little with the rising cost of living, up by almost 15 percent in the period from his inauguration to the summer of 1971. In fact, the call for fiscal restraint, tight money policy, and high interest rates ran alongside an unprecedented situation in which high unemployment *and* inflation existed. Added to this, the trade deficit in 1971 placed new and serious strains on the U.S. balance of payments, which reached a deficit of nearly $30 billion, and for the first time in the twentieth century the nation's balance of trade (exports less imports) ran in the red to the tune of $3 billion.

Clearly, something had to be done. And done it was. On August 15 President Nixon imposed a ninety-day freeze on prices, wages, and rents in order to halt inflation. Phase I, the first of such controls in peacetime, was accompanied by the suspension of the convertibility of the dollar into gold, a 10 percent surcharge on imports, and a 10 percent reduction in foreign aid. During the course of the "New Economic Policy," inflation fell from 3.8 percent to 1.9 percent while unemployment fell from 6.1 percent to 5.1 percent by the end of 1972. Other tax changes designed to stimulate the economy, together with an expansionary fiscal policy, became law in December. Gradually phased out by the end of 1974, the Nixon wage and price controls, deemed politically necessary, proved popular in the short term. "But in the long run," reflected Nixon in his memoirs, "I believe it was wrong. The piper must always be paid, and there was an unquestionably high price for tampering with the orthodox economic mechanism." Few believed the president's conversion to Keynesianism was anything but expedient. His commitment to lowering taxes, freeing agriculture of almost all production controls (realized in 1973), and abolishing controls on international capital movements more clearly mirrored his Republican training than anything else.

Toward a New Republican Conservative Majority

A minority president, with only 43 percent of the total votes, Nixon struggled to create a new majority, including liberals and antiwar factions of both parties, in his first years in office. Despite apparent efforts to talk "consensus politics" and to lower voices, Nixon failed to impress either the liberal press, which did not really believe he was trying to get out of Vietnam, or liberals in the Senate who among other things rejected his Supreme Court nominations. At this point, and for reasons of its own, the administration changed tack, reverting to partisan and ideological attacks on the president's opponents.

In the name of the "silent majority," peace with honor in Vietnam, and law and order, the president set loose Vice-President Agnew to impugn the programs and honor of the opposition in anticipation of the 1970 congressional election. No stranger to controversy—a year earlier Agnew had assailed liberal-leaning electronic media coverage as the work of a "small band of network commentators"—the vice-president lashed out at "radical liberals" and other "nattering nabobs of negativism." The election results were mixed with the GOP losing nine seats in the House while picking up two in the Senate; the overall effect of Nixon's efforts, according to *New York Times* writer James Reston, "revived all the old doubts about his [Nixon's] political and personal prejudices, restored all his old battles with the press, and raised the kind of credibility gap that destroyed President Johnson." He even managed to unify the Democrats, never an easy thing.

In his third State of the Union Message, delivered to Congress on January 22, 1971, Nixon introduced the concept of revenue sharing—putting money where the needs were greatest, putting power to spend it where the people were. As a gesture toward efficiency and a nod to the increasing restiveness of state legislatures, the president asked Congress to set a target of giving state and local governments at least $16 billion annually in order "to close the gap between promise and performance" at all levels of government. The distribution of power was not in question. Under the scheme, approximately one-third of the Federal domestic grant program would be placed in a revenue-sharing fund and, from there, dispersed to local and state governments for expenditure under six broad categories: urban development, rural development, education, transportation, manpower training, and law enforcement.

This highly touted proposal took shape in October 1972 in the form of a five-year Revenue Sharing Act designed to distribute $30.2 billion of Federal tax revenue to state and local governments as supplements to their own revenues, to use generally as they saw fit. The bill, signed into law just two weeks before the presidential election, comprised an important part of the "next American revolution" that the administration had promised the nation. Since 1972, $64.9 billion has been disbursed to help pay for a multitude of goods and services, ranging from day-care centers to mass transport.

The Democratic National Convention, meeting in Miami in the second week in July, nominated fifty-year-old Senator George S. McGovern of South Dakota as candidate for president. A mainstream Democrat, longtime opponent of the Vietnam War, and a major figure in restructuring the party's selection processes and convention procedures, McGovern easily swept aside challenges from Senator Hubert Humphrey of Minnesota and Edmund Muskie of Maine. Defying the polls and the odds, the former historian presided over a convention whose delegate selection process was open to all enrolled party members and whose composition reflected the proportionate representation of minorities, women, and the young. For his running mate McGovern chose Thomas F. Eagleton, a freshman senator from St. Louis, Missouri. An urbane and highly personable lawyer, the forty-two-year-old Eagleton withdrew from the ticket in late July when it was learned that he had had a history of psychiatric treatment. The Democratic National Committee, at a special meeting held in August, agreed to McGovern's seventh choice for the post, R. Sargent Shriver, former director of the Peace Corps.

The theme of the McGovern campaign was "Come Home America"—

home from war in remote places, home from the errant path of wasteful military spending, wasteful unemployment, pandering to special interests, and deception in high places. The latter referred to the break-in of the offices of the Democratic National Committee, located in the Watergate, an apartment-hotel complex in Washington, on June 17,1972, on the eve of the nominating convention. Though this so-called third-rate burglary would have no impact on the campaign, subsequently revealed links between the five men apprehended and White House consultant E. Howard Hunt and counsel to the Committee to Reelect the President (CREEP) G. Gordon Liddy, would open the door to a series of scandals reaching up to the Oval Office.

Assembling in Miami in late August, the Republican National Convention jubilantly nominated the president as the GOP's leader for the third time in twelve years. Spiro Agnew easily won reendorsement as vice-president. Nixon, in a polished and orchestrated convention, summoned Americans, particularly the young, the old, and disaffected Democrats, to join his "new majority." "I ask everyone listening to me tonight," said the president, drawing a sharp contrast between himself and his liberal challanger, "Democrats, Republicans and independents, to join our new majority, not on the basis of the party label you wear on your lapel but what you believe in your hearts." Nixon pressed the argument that the nation faced the clearest choice of the twentieth century—the 1964 election between Goldwater and Lyndon Johnson apparently having been less so. Furthermore, the choice would not be "between radical change and no change" but between "change that works and change that won't work"—the prudent use of world power or return to isolationism, peace with honor in Vietnam or appeasement, economic growth or stagnation, quality education for all or arbitrary racial balance.

The result of the campaign, which was marked by a minimum of personal appearances by the president and a seeming inability on the part of McGovern to rid himself of his fuzzy image, ended in a landslide for Nixon: 47,169,911 (60.6 percent) to 29,170,383 (37.5 percent). A major factor in the outcome was a massive shift to the GOP of the traditionally Democratic blue-collar workers in northern cities who, according to one Gallup poll analysis, feared McGovern would encourage a permissive society that would accordingly fail to provide safe streets and cities; another factor was the preference given to the administration by the supporters of Governor George C. Wallace whose own run for the presidency ended in May when a would-be assassin's bullet paralyzed him. In any case, and despite the poor showing in the congressional elections—a net gain of thirteen seats in the House and the loss of two seats in the Senate—the president could well assume that his new conservative majority had finally arrived.

"Years of Upheaval"

President Nixon's second term in office was, in the words of Henry Kissinger (who replaced William Rogers as secretary of state in September 1973), a time of upheaval without precedent in the nation's history. For, commented Kissinger, "a president fresh from the second largest electoral victory in our history was unseated in a revolution that his own actions had triggered and his conduct could not quell. . . . We had begun . . . imagining that we were on the threshold of a creative new era in international affairs. . . . Within weeks we confronted a nightmarish collapse of authority at home and a desperate struggle to keep foreign adversaries from transforming it into an assault on our nation's security and that of other free peoples." The nightmare the former professor of government referred to in his memoir was the Watergate scandal which in itself became a symbol of a wide range of illegal actions and misconduct in high places, from the conspiracy to cover up the original Watergate burglary to presidential impoundment of Federal funds, to wiretap and political spying, to perjury and bribery, to illegal campaign contributions, to illegally authorized bombing of targets in Indochina.

According to White House tape recordings (a recording system had been installed in early 1971), it is certain that as early as June 23, 1972, the president and his chief aide and former advertising man, H. R. Haldeman, had conspired to block further FBI investigations into the Watergate case. Other efforts to cover up the burglary included raising money to buy the silence of the defendants who were indicted in September, and perjury before the grand jury by the deputy director of CREEP, Jeb Stuart Magruder. The investigative reporting of *Washington Post* journalists Bob Woodward and Carl Bernstein, which tied ex-Attorney General John Mitchell to a secret fund to finance intelligence operations against the Democrats, was written off by White House press spokesman Ronald Ziegler as "the shoddiest kind of journalism."

In January 1973, the actual Watergate trial began before Judge John J. Sirica, chief judge of the U.S. District Court for the District of Columbia, who personally interrogated defense witnesses. Though two of the defendants were convicted by a jury, Sirica expressed doubt that the whole story had been determined and called for further investigation.

On February 7, a month before Watergate operative John W. McCord revealed that others had been involved and two months before Haldeman and fellow White House aide John D. Ehrlichman (a former Seattle zoning lawyer) had been abandoned by Nixon, the Senate established a seven-man Select Committee on Presidential Campaign Activities. Senator Sam Ervin of North Carolina was appointed as chairman. Before long, the televised public hearings brought the Watergate affair high public visibility, touching on the origins of a White House "Enemies List" of administration critics, secret funds, a "dirty tricks" unit, and the knowledge, disclosed by Alexander Butterfield, former deputy presidential assistant, that the president had tape recorded all his conversations in the White House and Executive Office Building.

In the meantime Nixon appointed Elliott Richardson as his third attorney general and Professor Archibald Cox of the Harvard Law School as his administration's own special prosecutor. Asserting executive privilege, the president refused to release the tapes either to Cox or the Ervin Committee; Judge Sirica then ordered the chief executive to turn over the tapes to him on August 29, a decision upheld in a higher court in October. After Professor Cox turned down a compromise whereby written summaries of the tapes would be verified by Senator John C. Stennis of Mississippi, Nixon had Cox fired, despite the protests and resignation of the attorney general and deputy attorney general. The "Saturday Night Massacre" of October 20 led to general public condemnation of Nixon.

Events that followed included the decision of Nixon to obey Judge Sirica's order to hand over some of the tapes, to the introduction of sixteen impeachment resolutions in the House of Representatives, and the appointment of Senator William Saxbe of Ohio as the next attorney general and Houston attorney Leon Jaworski as the next special prosecutor. Of the nine tapes requested by Judge Sirica, two were claimed by the White House never to have existed and a third had a sinister gap of eighteen minutes, subsequently determined to be the work of multiple erasures. Disclosure of the tapes revealed more and more shady characters and low thinking in high places.

To make matters worse, Vice-President Spiro Agnew resigned on October 9, 1973, after entering a plea of "no contest" in a U.S. District Court in Baltimore to a charge that he had failed to report payments (that is, bribes) from Maryland contractors on his 1967 income tax return. U.S. District Judge Walter E. Hoffman, apparently moved by the tragic sight of the erstwhile vice-president of the United States throwing himself on the mercy of his court, placed Agnew on probation for three years and fined him

$10,000. (In 1982, Maryland's Court of Appeals, the state's highest court, ordered Agnew to pay the state $147,500 for kickbacks he purportedly received from highway contractors from 1967 to 1969, plus $101,235 in interest, the state ultimately upholding the suit of three Maryland taxpayers that Agnew be held accountable for his illegal actions. (A payment of nearly $270,000, including interest, was made to the Maryland Treasury in 1983.) Under the terms of the Twenty-Fifth Amendment, ratified in 1967 and never used previously, Gerald Ford of Michigan, minority leader of the House of Representatives, was nominated by Nixon two days later to be the fortieth vice-president of the United States. Within the next two weeks, Ford was overwhelmingly confirmed both in the House and the Senate. For the moment at least Congress and the president could agree on one thing.

Two weeks before the "Saturday Night Massacre," on October 6, 1973, the Day of Atonement—the holiest day in the Jewish calendar—the fourth Arab-Israeli War since 1948 broke out. The Arab attack, led by an Egyptian offensive across the Suez Canal and a Syrian offensive on the Golan Heights, took the Israeli government of Prime Minister Golda Meir totally by surprise. On both fronts the Arabs, fighting with a determination and spirit that fully redeemed the image of the Arab soldier of 1967, met with initial success only to be checked by an Israeli counteroffensive on both the Egyptian and Syrian frontiers. In the former action, Israeli forces achieved a bridgehead on the west bank of the Suez Canal, reaching to within seventy miles of Cairo, managing to encircle the Egyptian Third Army of twenty thousand soldiers on the east bank; in the latter situation, the Israelis had managed to reconquer the whole of the Golan Heights and advanced to within twenty miles of Damascus.

Washington's response to the conflict was a measured one, consisting mainly of matching Soviet arms to its clients and persuading Moscow to assist in effecting a U.N.-sponsored ceasefire. On October 13 the administration began replenishing Israeli war stocks, while a week later Congress approved $2.2 billion in aid. The Arab response, lasting until March 1974, was to initiate an oil embargo against the United States.

The first great oil shock of the 1970s exerted a disastrous effect on the American economy, far beyond higher prices for gasoline, home heating, and fuel oil. During the first quarter of 1974 the gross national product of the United States declined 6.3 percent, marking, according to most economic analysts, the end of a post-World War II era of high growth rates and full employment for the industrialized world. After diplomatic skirmishing, the belligerents agreed to a U.N. ceasefire on October 24. Meanwhile, President Nixon had to exert tremendous pressure on the Soviet Union, principally by placing American troops around the world on alert status, after having considered using nuclear weapons, to dissuade the Kremlin from dispatching an expeditionary force to the area to bring about an observance of the ceasefire. The Soviet leadership grasped the message, and the crisis was dissipated when the U.N. Security Council called for the creation of an emergency force exclusive of the permanent members of the Council.

At the conclusion of the fighting, there occurred a spate of diplomatic activities aimed at laying the foundation for a more lasting peace in the Middle East. The most important of these efforts included Secretary of State Kissinger's mission to the area in November, resulting not only in the resumption of diplomatic relations with Cairo for the first time since 1967, but also in the signing of an Egyptian-Israeli ceasefire instrument on November 11, the first major agreement between Israel and an Arab state since 1949. In January 1974 the secretary achieved a partial Egyptian-Israeli disengagement understanding in the Sinai, completed in September 1975. And, in May 1974, he organized a disengagement pact between Syria and Israel in the strategic Golan Heights. These gains for peace were the consequence of Kissinger's so-called shuttle diplomacy, estimated at keeping the secretary away from Washington for the average of approximately one out of every six weeks during 1974 and 1975. Still, a comprehensive peace settlement continued to elude Kissinger.

The Arab oil embargo, with its real threat to the nation's energy needs, made the American winter of 1973–1974 a winter of political discontent. On November 7, 1973, the president announced on television what he called the "stark fact" that the nation was faced with the most acute shortage of energy since World War II. To meet the crisis he ordered, as a symbolic gesture, heat to be lowered in Federal buildings to between 65 and 68 degrees fahrenheit; asked Congress to give him authority to relax environmental restrictions; asked that the country be returned to daylight-savings time; and called for the imposition of a nationwide speed limit of fifty-five miles per hour on Federal highway systems. These latter two proposals were quickly made into law. In his January 1974 State of the Union Message, the president asserted that, "the number one legislative concern must be the energy crisis."

Despite the best efforts of conservation, lines of automobiles at gas stations lengthened, suppliers invariably ran low, and the price of gasoline soared. All of this, including the gloom-and-doom predictions of instant experts, led to greater inflation and economic recession. As the crisis eased, Americans increasingly looked about for alternative energy sources while continuing to place stock in such legislation as the Trans-

Alaska Oil Pipeline projected to supply the United States with an additional two million barrels of oil per day by 1980. In any case and whatever theory of the oil conspiracy one believed—it appeared to some observers that gasoline "shortages" began in the boardrooms of the oil giants at home—life in America, with its love affair with the automobile, would never be quite the same again.

The Nixon Resignation

The impeachment resolutions of October 1973 were duly handed over to the House Judiciary Committee, headed by Democratic Congressman Peter Rodino of New Jersey. Rodino, granted broad powers of subpoena, began closed hearings in May 1974, two months after a grand jury indicted the former attorney general and several of his closest aides, all of whom were subsequently convicted; Nixon was himself cited as an unindicted co-conspirator in the Watergate cover-up. In response to requests to turn over additional tape recordings, the president gambled by releasing a number of them himself. It was a blunder as the recordings once again depicted the president in the worst kind of light. By late July, 51 percent of the American public had reached the conclusion that there was indeed enough evidence to bring Nixon to trial before the Senate, the final step in impeachment proceedings.

And so did the House Judiciary Committee which, between July 25 and July 30, after televised debate, voted three articles of impeachment. Specifically, the committee found that President Nixon (1) had "prevented, obstructed, and impeded the administration of justice"; (2) had "repeatedly engaged in conduct violating the constitutional rights of citizens, impairing the due and proper administration of justice in the conduct of lawful inquiries, or contravening the laws governing agencies of the executive branch"; and (3) had "failed without lawful cause or excuse to produce papers and things, as directed by duly authorized subpoenas . . . thereby assuming for himself functions and judgments necessary to the exercise of the sole power of impeachment vested by the Constitution in the House of Representatives." For such offenses, concluded Rodino's committee, "Richard M. Nixon . . . warrants impeachment and trial, and removal from office."

On August 5, with time running out, Nixon finally yielded the incriminating tapes of June 23, 1972, revealing beyond doubt that he had played a significant role in the cover-up. With the emergence of the proverbial "smoking gun," it became apparent that the chief executive had lost the support of all but his most resolute supporters in the Senate, probably no more than fifteen members, according to Senator Goldwater. Facing the inevitable, and with the prospect of a trial, conviction, prison sentence, and loss of his Federal pension before him, the thirty-seventh president of the United States announced on the evening of August 8 that he was abandoning his fight to remain in office and would resign the next day.

At 11:35 AM on August 9, the moment Nixon's letter of resignation was turned over to the secretary of state, Vice-President Gerald Ford assumed the power of the presidency. Then, shortly after noon, President Ford took the oath of office from Chief Justice Warren Burger in the historic East Room of the White House. "Our long national nightmare," declared the new chief executive, "is over." Richard Nixon departed Washington in disgrace.

The aftermath of the Watergate scandal left its mark on the course and quality of American politics and government. The congressional response alone resulted in a spate of legislation designed to establish new standards of ethics and accountability for holders of the public trust (campaign financing and budget laws, the latter to prevent a chief executive from "impounding" appropriated moneys), to curb presidential authority abroad (the War Powers Act, forcing the president to keep Congress apprised of the commitment of U.S. troops to foreign hostilities), and to institutionalize procedures for the appointment of a special prosecutor to investigate charges brought against high administration officials. Lessons abounded. According to Barbara Jordan, former Congresswoman (Democrat, Texas) who played a prominent role in the impeachment proceedings: "Because of Watergate, I think public officials have become much more sensitive to the demands and requirements of their jobs." According to politicial scientist James Barber, "We damn well ought to pay more attention to who we put in the White House."

Two long-term effects, argued influential television correspondent Walter Cronkite elsewhere, included, first, a national cynicism about government on all levels and, second, diminished public regard for the press. Though it took the participants themselves a long time to recognize it, because of their euphoria over running Nixon to ground, concluded Cronkite, the massive assault launched on the press in the early 1970s and spearheaded by Vice-President Spiro Agnew had taken its toll in the form of lessening public respect for the media.

And, finally, one might well ask, what of Richard Nixon? What had a man resoundingly returned to office hoped to achieve? Liberals believed then and now that he had hoped, in the words of critic Mary McCarthy, "to dismantle the Constitution, not only its rights and guarantees but its essential tripartite structure," i.e., the division of power between the executive, legislative, and judicial branches of government. Still others have surmised that the former president's disdain for the Constitution differed only marginally from the typical mentality that informed corporate America; put another way, Nixon's view of the true, the good, and the beautiful differed little from that of the people who swept him into office.

Still unrepentant, Nixon finally came to admit that the break-in by the Watergate "plumbers" was both illegal and, he remarked in 1984, "a very, very stupid thing to do." He also went on to describe the bungled cover-up organized by his administration as "stupidity at the very highest," and concluded by condemning his own failure to destroy the incriminating Watergate tapes before they were subpoenaed by the investigation panel. Such an action would probably have saved his presidency though weakened the Republic, perhaps beyond repair. In the end, Nixon's insecure personality, together with an extraordinary set of sycophantic advisers, proved the undoing of the nation's chief executive who by all common measurements would surely have gone to jail in other circumstances. The price of placing one's friends above the interests of the Republic would always be a heavy one for the occupant of the Oval Office. Richard Nixon paid that price.

Suggested Readings

Agnew, Spiro. *Go Quietly. . . or else.* 1980.
Bell, Coral. *The Diplomacy of Détente: the Kissinger Era.* 1977.
Bernstein, Carl and Woodward, Robert. *All the President's Men.* 1974.
Brodie, Fawn M. *Richard Nixon: The Shaping of His Character.* 1981.
Dean, John W. *Blind Ambition.* 1976.
Haldeman, H.R. *The Ends of Power.* 1978.
Kissinger, Henry. *White House Years.* 1979.
_____. *Years of Upheaval.* 1982.
Moynihan, Daniel P. *The Politics of a Guaranteed Income.* 1973.
Nixon, Richard M. *RN: The Memoirs of Richard Nixon.* 1968.
Phillips, Kevin P. *The Emerging Republican Majority.* 1969.
Porter, Gareth. *A Peace Denied.* 1975.
Quandt, William B. *Decade of Decision: American Foreign Policy toward the Arab-Israeli Conflict, 1967–1976.* 1978.
Safire, William. *Before the Fall.* 1975.
Schlesinger, Arthur M. *The Imperial Presidency.* 1973.
Shawcross, William. *Sideshow: Kissinger, Nixon and the Destruction of Cambodia.* 1975.

Silk, Leonard. *Nixonomics*. 1972.
Szulk, Tad. *The Illusion of Peace: Foreign Policy in the Nixon Years*. 1978.
White, Theodore H. *The Making of the President, 1972*. 1973.
Wills, Garry. *Nixon Agonistes*. 1970.

6

A Time for Healing: From Gerald Ford To Jimmy Carter

Gerald R. Ford first saw the light of day as Leslie King, Jr. on July 14, 1913, in Omaha, Nebraska. When he was a child, his mother divorced his father and settled in Grand Rapids, Michigan, where she met and married Gerald Ford, a local businessman, who adopted the youngster and gave him his name.

Ford was graduated in 1935 from the University of Michigan (where he distinguished himself as a member [linesman] of national championship football teams) and from the Yale Law School in 1941; academically, he was in the upper third of his class at both universities. After spending World War II in the navy and practicing law in his home town of Grand Rapids, he was elected to the House of Representatives in 1948. He served there consecutively for twenty-five years, reaching the position of minority leader in 1965, until his appointment as vice-president.

Well-liked, hard-working, and conservative, Congressman Ford opposed measures such as minimum wage bills, the establishment of the Office of Economic Opportunity, and Medicare; he supported legislation aimed at building the controversial supersonic transport plane (SST), prohibiting the busing of school children, and impeaching controversial Supreme Court Justice William O. Douglas. He ultimately succeeded to the presidency, according to political observer Richard Reeves, because he managed to make himself "the least objectionable alternative." For himself, Ford was "acutely aware that you have not elected me as your president by your ballots." And while he took pride in being "a Ford, not a Lincoln," he also had no doubts that he was "not a Model T." "I have old-fashioned ideas," the new president declared to an enthusiastic joint session of Congress only three days after he took office, "I believe in the basic decency and fairness of America."

The Ghost of Watergate

The president's first order of business was to name Governor Nelson Rockefeller of New York, leader of the liberal wing of the Republican party and perennial aspirant to the White House, as his vice-president. His second order of business was to let his predecessor off the proverbial hook. On September 8, 1974, and despite his own, earlier comment, "I do not think the public would stand for it," President Ford granted former President Richard Nixon "a full, free, and absolute pardon . . . for all offenses against the United States which he . . . has committed or may have committed or taken part in during the period from January 20, 1969, through August 9, 1974." The nation was stunned as Nixon observed with perhaps no little understatement that "I was wrong in not acting more decisively and more forthrightly in dealing with Watergate." Reactions to the pardon, whose rationale was to spare Nixon and the nation further punishment, fell mainly, though not entirely, along party lines. Not surprisingly, the congressional mid-term election in November reflected the verdict of the average American when the Democrats were returned to the House (291 to 144) and the Senate (61 to 37) with overwhelming majorities. Ford's honeymoon with Congress had come to an abrupt end.

Government by Veto

Unable to command enough congressional support to press his own economic programs, and with tight money policy producing high interest rates, and with the impact of the quadrupling of the price of oil hard upon the economy, President Ford presided over the worst recession since the Great Depression. Despite the increasing availability of gasoline, by 1975 unemployment had reached the 9 percent mark, with more than one million jobs lost in that year; inflation rose to 12 percent, dropping to less than 5 percent in 1976, mainly at the expense of bringing the growth of the economy to a halt.

The administration and the 94th Congress were at loggerheads from the outset. Opposed to the expansionist monetary policies of the Democrats and unable to push through any legislation of his own, Ford turned to an unprecedented use of the presidential veto. At different times the former minority leader vetoed a $5.3 billion package designed to fund job-producing projects across the nation on the grounds that, "it would exacerbate both budgetary and economic pressures," and a $7.9 billion aid-to-education bill on the grounds it was unsound and would "authorize excessive appropriation levels." All in all, the president resorted to the veto more than sixty times. More positively, Ford signed into law the Energy Policy and Conservation Act of 1975, deregulating the price of oil among other things and the Energy Reorganiztion Bill of the same year, setting up an Energy Research and Development Administration. In 1976 he issued an executive order restricting the power of the Central Intelligence Agency to intrude upon the lives and activities of American citizens.

The End of Détente

With Henry Kissinger in charge of the State Department, President Ford generally continued to pursue the foreign policy goals of the Nixon administration. A major breakthrough was in fact reached in the second phase of the SALT II negotiations at a meeting in Vladivostok in November 1974 between Ford and Soviet General Secretary Brezhnev. With a view to striking a compromise between the Soviet advantage in numbers of strategic launchers permitted by the temporary five-year accord and America's three-to-one advantage in multiple nuclear warheads, the two sides agreed to an overall limit of 2,400 strategic nuclear delivery vehicles; 1,320 on MIRV systems; a ban on the construction of new land-based ICBM launchers; and limits on the deployment of new types of strategic offensive areas. It soon became clear, however, that fundamental disagreement remained with respect to whether the new Soviet bomber (code-named Backfire) would be considered a heavy bomber and thus counted in the 2,400 overall total.

On another front, the president travelled to Helsinki in late summer 1975 to sign, along with the heads of the thirty-five nations of Europe, the so-called final act of the Conference on Security and Cooperation in Europe. The high-water mark of détente, the Helsinki Conference declared the current frontiers of Europe "inviolable," thereby endorsing the Soviet Union's post-World War II territorial gains, as well as its hegemony in Eastern Europe. In return, the administration hoped to induce Moscow to open its East European empire to a freer flow of people and ideas, reaffirming the

ideal of the dignity of the individual. There was no shortage of critics of détente in the United States—western Europeans tended to have a more sanguine outlook on the matter—to point out that communist-dominated police
states seldom work this way. Détente seemed to such notables as diplomat
George F. Kennan and Soviet dissident and Nobel prize winner in literature
Aleksandar Solzhenitsyn—not to mention the pack of Democrats running
for office in 1976—a one-way street.

To make matters worse, evidence on all sides indicated that Moscow
had abandoned the conventional rules of the game. Through use of East German and Cuban surrogates, the Soviet Union threw its weight behind the leftist regime in the Angolian Civil War, begun in 1975, indicating a new, more
belligerent Soviet approach to the Third World. Cribbed and confined by
congressional resolutions barring American involvement *of any kind* in the
conflict, the administration could only protest that Moscow's presence there
was "harmful" to détente. Perhaps more significant was the public revelation
of the CIA's assessment of Soviet defense spending in 1976; according to the
study, the percentage of the USSR's gross national product absorbed by defense spending had increased from 6 to 8 percent to 11 to 13 percent. Media
reports that the CIA had "doubled" its estimate of Soviet defense expenditures sent shock waves through the national intelligence community. (That
the figures may have also reflected a heightened American appreciation of
how far less efficient Soviet defense industries were than formerly believed—"less bang for the ruble"—seems not to have interested the attentive
public.) Kissinger's strategy of weaving a web of interconnections, whose
benefits might seem important enough to the Kremlin to restrain itself, appeared to have lost its rationale and became identified with being "soft" on
the Soviet Union.

About the only positive achievement the administration's foreign policy had to show for itself was the retaking of the American ship, the
Mayagüez, in May 1975, from Cambodian communists who apparently had
not counted on the president to send in the marines. The success of the operation was applauded throughout the nation, and it enhanced Ford's stature in
the White House.

"Why Not the Best?"

The Democratic National Convention, meeting in New York for the first
time in more than fifty years, nominated outsider and political moderate
Governor James (Jimmy) Earl Carter, Jr., of Georgia by an overwhelming

margin on the first ballot. Determined, efficient, and luckier than most, Carter began his campaign in 1972, midway through his gubernatorial administration. Born in Plains, Georgia, on October 1, 1924, of modest circumstances, Jimmy Carter appeared a man of a thousand faces, the Lon Chaney of 1976. He was at once, in the words of his campaign autobiography, *Why Not the Best?*, a Southerner (the first major party nominee from the Deep South since LBJ from Texas), an American, a peanut farmer, an engineer (a graduate of the U.S. Naval Academy in 1946), a father and a husband, a born-again Christian, a politician and former governor, a planner, a businessman, a nuclear physicist, a naval officer, a canoeist and, among other things, a lover of Bob Dylan's songs and Dylan Thomas's poetry.

He was above all the consummate technician. Cultivating the simple virtues of honesty, decency, and competency, Carter touched the nation's raw nerve when he told the assembled delegation that "It's now a time for healing. We want to have faith again. We want to be proud again. We just want the truth again." At the convention, Carter chose liberal Senator Walter F. Mondale of Minnesota as his running mate. In the domestic sphere, the party platform rested on means to fight unemployment through public works projects and financial incentives to private enterprise, welfare reform, tax reform, and in extensive and mandatory national health insurance programs; in the foreign affairs and defense spheres, rejection of détente to be replaced by "hard bargaining" with the Soviet Union, a $5.7 billion cut in defense spending, a comprehensive Middle East peace settlement, normalization of relations with Peking, and "more openness" in foreign policy making.

At the Republican National Convention, held at Kansas City in August, Gerald Ford was nominated in his own right on the first ballot. Ford, who had struggled for seven grueling months to beat off the challenge of Republican conservative Governor Ronald Reagan of California, a popular movie actor-turned politician, selected Senator Robert J. Dole of Kansas as his running mate. A member of the House of Representatives for four terms, a senator since 1969, and one of Nixon's strongest supporters, Dole's appointment could only be explained as appeasement of the growing Reaganite right wing of the Republican party. The GOP platform opposed national health insurance preferring instead to expand Medicare payments to hospitals; concentrated on fiscal means to reduce inflation; advocated expansion of Nixon's revenue-sharing program with the states; pledged to keep up U.S. might while still trying to negotiate strategic arms limitations with Moscow (with the use of the word *détente* disappearing from the language); and sought the continuance of Kissinger's "step-by-step" approach toward a Middle East peace solution.

The highlight of the campaign, which was otherwise undistinguished, were the three presidential debates held between the candidates in September and October; these were the first television debates ever between an incumbent and a challenger. They were also decisive. The second debate, held on foreign policy issues, witnessed the president's unaccountable gaffe regarding the status of nations locked in the Soviet Eastern European empire—they were independent of Moscow—as well as the hightide of the rival's challenge. For his part, Carter found support and votes in claiming to be an anti-Washington, anti-establishment figure, not a lawyer, not a liar. Probably his trump card was his claim that he told the truth and that he would never lie to the American people. "If I ever lie to you, if I ever mislead you, if I ever avoid a controversial issue, don't vote for me," he said. Thus, in the view of one close observer, "Carter cornered the truth market early in a year when the voters sought, above all else, an honest politician"—the kind of candidate the post-Watergate times demanded. He was also fuzzy on the major *public* issues, in fact almost edgy about them, saying on one occasion, "I don't give a damn about abortion or amnesty or right to work laws. . . . They're impossible political issues."

The formula worked well enough when on polling day Carter snatched the presidency from his opponent with a popular vote count of 40,276,040 (50.1 percent) to 38,532,630 (48 percent) and an electoral score of 291 to 241. Furthermore, the Democrats held their two-to-one margin in the House of Representatives (292–144) and led in the Senate (61–38, plus the independent Senator Harry Byrd of Virginia). After eight years in the wilderness, the Democrats could look with confidence to working with a chief executive who had reunited the basic elements of Franklin D. Roosevelt's New Deal coalition: organized labor, minorities, urban dwellers, the aged, and committed liberals.

Jimmy Carter in the White House

"I have no new dream to set forth today," declared the thirty-ninth president of the United States at his inauguration on January 20, 1977, "but rather urge a fresh faith in the old dream. . . . Let us create together a new national spirit of unity and trust." Generally, President Carter, a deacon in the Southern Baptist Church with a penchant for quoting Old Testament prophets, committed his administration to enhancing equality of opportunity, to preserving the nation's natural beauty, to fostering respect for human rights home and abroad, to keeping the nation strong militarily, to eliminating nuclear weapons from the face of the earth and, before all else, to recognizing the nation's limits in being able to solve all problems much less afford to do everything. Then, in a break with tradition and in sharp contrast to the style of Nixon's "Imperial Presidency," Carter and his family walked the entire mile and a half in subfreezing weather from the Capitol to the White House. The other symbolic action on his first day in office was to pardon, by executive order, all draft evaders of the Vietnam War, which with Watergate, the president was anxious to relegate to the past.

President Carter's major cabinet appointments reflected varying degrees of geographical diversity and breadth of experience: Cyrus Vance of New York, secretary of state; Harold Brown of California, secretary of defense; Michael Blumenthal of Michigan, secretary of the treasury; and Zbigniew Brzezinski of New York, national security adviser. To this level, the fifty-two year old Democrat added the names of fellow Georgians Bert Lance, director of the Office of Management and Budget; Griffin Bell, attorney general; and Andrew Young, ambassador to the United Nations. (Lance, an Atlanta banker, resigned under a financial cloud in September 1977.) The bulk of the White House staff, led by political strategist Hamilton Jordan and Press Secretary Jody Powell, originated from Georgia as well.

In nearly twenty-five hundred speeches and hundreds of interviews during a two-year presidential campaign, candidate Carter promised many programs, reforms, and changes, frequently adding the phrase, "and you can depend on that." In fact, it required his aides several weeks to compile the president's more than six hundred promises in a 110-page book, soon dubbed "Promises, Promises," after a popular Broadway musical. When he entered office, Carter was of the opinion that unemployment rather than inflation was the main domestic issue. Among his campaign promises the president promised to reduce the military budget, curtail arms sales abroad, balance the budget by 1981, restrain the spread of nuclear weapons, free Americans of their "inordinate fear of communism," bring stability to the Middle East, return the Panama Canal, protect the environment, and establish an effective energy policy. It was not long before public dissatisfaction set in, perhaps from expecting more than he, or anyone else, could have delivered. The cumulative effect of high inflation *and* high employment—despite the appointment of a tight-money advocate, Paul Volcker, to the chairmanship of the Federal Reserve Board—high costs of living, of housing, of borrowing money, and of his overstating the threat of the Afghan crisis (which he described as the most serious confrontation for the United States with the Soviet Union since 1945) took its toll. Carter became within a short time the most unpopular president since Herbert Hoover, widely regarded as incompetent, indecisive, and uninspiring.

Perhaps it was a bad time for the Georgian to be president. Americans increasingly expected more of their leaders; they demanded simple answers, simple solutions. There were none of these. Other matters handicapped President Carter in his efforts to be an effective chief executive. These factors included public mistrust of presidential leadership, diverse special-interest groups and, especially, the growing independence of Congress. Despite the heavy Democratic majorities, the president seemed unable to lead Congress, much less control it; even with the successes he had, there was nearly always more than the usual struggle between the White House and Capitol Hill.

Moreover, there was, and remains, the intractability of the nation's problems, possibly Carter's greatest handicap. Major problems such as inflation and energy were not of the Georgian's making, and his proposals to deal with them did not bring striking results, though, to be certain, there were some notable achievements. Other political leaders, many of whom had been frustrated in their own recent bid to occupy the Oval Office, failed to come up with better solutions. And finally, but equally troublesome for the president, was the reluctance of Americans everywhere to subordinate local interests to national need.

"One cannot fairly assess Jimmy Carter as President," remarked the *New York Times* in June 1979, "without assessing the self-interested people and baffling problems over which he presides." And as James Reston pointed out about the Washington outsider who once lost his way to the Oval Office and delighted in throwing frisbees on the White House ground, "He came to town . . . promising to produce a 'Government as good and generous and unselfish as our people' and on the whole he has kept his promise. Maybe the trouble is that 'the people' are not quite as good and generous and unselfish as he thought."

According to his memoirs, Carter's primary thought on Inauguration Day was about the potential shortage of energy supplies and the need for the American people to stop looking to the Federal government as a bottomless cornucopia. "We desperately need," recalled the president, "a comprehensive program that would encourage conservation, more fuel production in the United States, and the long-range development of alternate forms of energy which could begin to replace oil and natural gas in future years." Furthermore, he continued, "these goals were complicated by the need to protect our environment, to insure equality of economic opportunity among the different regions of our country, and to balance the growing struggle between American consumers and oil producers." In an address to the nation on April 18, 1977, Carter likened the nation's struggle with the energy crisis to the "moral equivalent of war," a phrase coined by psychologist William James many years before and suggested to the president by Admiral Hyman Rickover, his role model and old boss in the nuclear-powered submarine fleet.

Conscious that the United States stood alone among the developed nations in being without an energy policy, the president struggled bitterly with Congress during the next three years, attaining most of what he sought. Essentially, the production of gasoline-inefficient automobiles was deterred by heavy penalties; electric utility companies could no longer encourage waste through their distorted rate structures, having also to join in a common effort to insulate buildings better; higher efficiency of home appliances was required; gasohol production and car pooling were promoted with tax incentives; coal production and use were stimulated together with the use of pollution control devices; and the carefully phased decontrol of natural gas prices war had begun. In addition, the president led the drive for the creation of the Department of Energy, coupled the decontrol of crude oil prices with a "windfall" profits tax designed to provide $227 billion in general revenues over ten years, and pushed through a program to develop synthetic fuel as an alternate source of energy. All in all, the administration could take pride in its energy achievements, though no one could guarantee that the mile-long gasoline line had become a thing of the past.

In other areas, the president promoted civil service reform, deregulated such key industries as airlines and trucking, and assisted in the birth of the Department of Education. In the field of environment, Carter rescued the Alaskan wilderness from haphazard development by persuading Congress to set aside 104.3 million acres of that state as environmentally protected lands, regulated strip mining of coal, and created a $1.6 billion fund to finance toxic waste disposal. (Disappointingly, by 1985, no long-term, permanent cleanup work had been started at 90 percent of the hazardous waste sites identified by the Environmental Protection Agency as the nation's most dangerous.) The administration had little success, however, in placing Social Security financing on a firmer footing, in instituting national health insurance, or in reforming welfare, affirmative action, or busing programs. Still, more members of racial minority groups were appointed to Federal positions than ever before.

The Women's Movement in the 1970s

During the decade of the 1970s, the women's liberation movement, the phrase itself taken from the Viet Cong and Black Liberation Movement, became, simply, the women's movement, a more benign term to encompass the variety of women's issues and the entire spectrum of women's beliefs. It was also designed to remove the aura of radicalism from the women's movement of the 1960s. The title change, which was never formally declared (by whom?—there was no acknowledged leader), symbolized a new hope that conspicuously absent groups such as black and Hispanic women would be recruited to the new movement, a goal that has not yet been realized.

The women's movement since congressional passage of the proposed Equal Rights Amendment (ERA), which would have prohibited discrimination based on sex by any law or action of government (federal, state, or local), has not had a single focus. There were just too many political, philosophical, and social differences among movement leaders. The multigenerational feature of the women's movement was preserved in the National Organization for Women (NOW), founded in 1966 by Betty Friedan, but in few of the other single-cause feminist groups.

Topics relating to women's sexuality, for example, occupied a great deal of attention within the women's movement: rape, abortion, and battered women all became highly publicized issues. The high incidence of rape in America (and Susan Brownmiller's historical study of the subject) had made rape counseling centers a major priority for many feminists. Similarly, many women lawyers worked with urban police departments to get them to treat women victims of rape respectfully and not to deprive them of their civil rights or their dignity. City councils passed legislation to deal with this issue as well.

Abortion has been one of the most controversial issues in the feminist debate for over a hundred years. Elizabeth Cady Stanton and Victoria Woodhull, earlier reformers, discussed this issue at women's meetings in the 1880s only to scandalize their Victorian sisters. Others such as Emma Goldman and Margaret Sanger were arrested for distributing birth control pamphlets in the early 1900s in New York City. Many later feminists argued that women had to have reproductive freedom and the right to end a pregnancy safely if all other forms of prevention failed.

In the 1960s the pill provided the first effective form of contraception for women, but many women could not afford the pill or could not take it without endangering their lives. In 1973, the Supreme Court ruled, in *Roe* v. *Wade,* that women had the legal right to an abortion in the first trimester of a pregnancy and in the second trimester under certain medically approved circumstances. The ruling was the first action that the Court had taken recognizing the woman's right to privacy and control over her own body. But the victory was severely restricted when, four years later, in *Beal* v. *Ann Doe,* the court ruled that states were not required to use public funds to perform abortions, thereby making it very difficult for poor women to fund abortions.

Although states could still fund welfare women's abortions, they were not compelled to do so, and in difficult economic times, many used this decision to deny women funds for that purpose. Indeed, the Supreme Court in the 1970s played the role of evaluator of much of the civil rights legislation that benefited women in the 1960s. Furthermore, its decisions have not always been clear.

For example, in the area of affirmative action programs (instituted to aid women and minorities obtain employment in areas where they had traditionally been discriminated against), the Court ruled in 1978 in *Bakke* v. *The Regents of the University of California* that Allan Bakke, a white applicant previously rejected by the University of California, be admitted to medical school but also held that "race" may be a factor in affirmative action programs at universities. In 1979, in *Weber* v. *Kaiser Aluminum,* the court upheld Kaiser's affirmative action program. There will surely be many more challenges to affirmative action programs in the future by white males charging discrimination—especially if the economy does not improve. These challenges endangered special efforts made by Federal agencies, education institutions, and private sector companies to recruit women into traditionally all-white, male job categories.

While the Court had been called upon to assess the meaning and constitutionality of legislation passed in the 1960s, Congress showed itself less ambitious in the area of women's rights. The most notable accomplishments included the 1972 Education Amendments, Title IX (which made it illegal to discriminate on the basis of sex in all public undergraduate institutions and in most private and public graduate and vocational schools receiving Federal monies), and the 1977 Equal Employment Opportunity Reorganization Act which, among other things, amended Title VII (of the Civil Rights Act), broadened EEOC jurisdiction to include the Equal Pay Act and the Age Discrimination Act. Otherwise, the Congress of the 1970s, consumed with Watergate in 1973–74, and a worsening economy after that, provided little in the way of social legislation generally and women's rights legislation particularly.

As noted the focus of the women's movement became more and more localistic and fragmented. Women's groups tended to work in their own communities to provide counseling for single mothers, battered women, rape victims, and pregnant teenagers. Though most of the groups supported ERA, the organization created to push for its passage found itself floundering after 1975. From 1972 to 1975, thirty-five of the needed thirty-eight states ratified the amendment, but then the movement lost its momentum. Representative Elizabeth Holtzman (Democrat, New York), with the support of President Carter, persuaded Congress to take the unprecedented step of extending the deadline for ratification by two years. Then, on June 30, 1982, the proposed Equal Rights Amendment to the Constitution died, three states shy of the number required for ratification. Foes of ERA led by Phyllis Schlafly, who contended that women were already protected by the 14th Amendment, offering equal protection to "all persons," and that such an amendment would cede states' rights to the Federal government, had won the latest, but doubtless not the last, round.

Despite the failure of ERA to pass, just as women's reform groups had focused upon local bases within which to work, so individual women went about improving their status in American society. The most notable example of success in this area was the increased education and professional entry of women into traditionally male-dominated fields. One has only to consider these figures:

	1960	1977
law	3.5%	9.5%
medicine	6.9%	11.2%
higher education	23.9%	31.7%
accounting	16.5%	27.5%
life & physical sciences	9.2%	15.6%

So, for the younger women coming of age in the 1970s and beyond, new professions were entered; indeed, more women went to college than ever before—in 1979, for the first time in American history, there were more women in colleges and universities than men. Obviously, older generations of women did not share in this good fortune, nor did many younger women of minority groups, most notably blacks and Hispanics whose infant mortality rate was about where the white rate was twenty-five years ago. But, all women's share of education was definitely on the increase at a faster pace than men's, and this factor suggested material changes in lifestyle and the character of the American family that would manifest themselves in the 1980s.

Women also had fewer children, delaying having the first child until their late 20s or early 30s, utilizing birth control methods, experimenting with different lifestyles, and generally living lives very different from their mothers' and grandmothers'. The longevity of American women allowed for comparisons never before made: sixty-year-old grandmothers could view their daughters' and granddaughters' lives and find themselves participating in aspects of the new feminism as well. Grandmothers worked part time and continued to be the backbone of volunteer organizations while their daughters returned to school and to careers, and their granddaughters contemplated becoming nuclear physicists.

At the same time, one could not avoid the observation that most American women still worked in sex-segregated fields: clerks and secretaries in offices and salespersons in shops represented the overwhelming majority of women workers. Though women had increased their share in professional work, they were clustered in education, social work, and librarianship. Administrators in schools, nursing schools, and social work schools were predominantly male. Women in the private sector slowly edged their way toward management positions by increasingly earning MBA degrees at major universities.

The goals of women's liberation, first articulated in the 1960s were (and are) slowly being enacted, sometimes in very different ways from the original intention. For example, 1960s feminist critiques of marriage expressed themselves among the populace as later entries into marriage, more divorces, and remarriages, fewer children, or childless marriages. Though "open" marriage was discussed frequently in the 1970s, monogamous marriage remained a value for most Americans. Redefinition and examination of marriage and the family, because of the women's movement, has not resulted in wholesale destruction of the institution, as feared by the critics; nor has it resulted in total reconstruction into communal or group marriage, as some feminists wished. Americans have in fact picked and chosen those aspects of feminist philosophies that appeared meaningful to them and applied and shaped them to their own unique needs, a typical example of a healthy cultural adjustment in a changing America.

The Hell of Good Intentions

The personnel, style, and emphasis on foreign policy of the Carter administration differed substantially from that of his recent predecessors. The so-

called Lone Ranger approach to international affairs, as presumably practiced by Henry Kissinger, was replaced by a more open, team-player concept espoused by Secretary of State Cyrus Vance, a corporate lawyer with
strong ties to the liberal eastern establishment. Other major actors included
National Security Adviser Zbigniew Brzezinski, a Polish-born Columbia
University professor specializing in Soviet affairs and the president's "ideas
man," and U.S. Ambassador to the United Nations Andrew Young, former
Georgia congressman and black civil rights activist, Carter's deputy to the
Third World.

More significantly, the president's commitment to the expansion of
human rights in nations ruled by totalitarian regimes (both of the left and the
right), together with his determination to press them at the expense of relations with the USSR and Latin American nations, set him apart from
the "power politics" or *Realpolitik* orientation of the preceding Nixon and
Ford administrations. "As President," recalled Carter, "I hoped and believed that the expansion of human rights might be the wave of the future
throughout the world, and I wanted the United States to be on the crest of this
movement.

Soon cognizant of pursuing such a policy too rigidly, the administration
came to define human rights on a number of levels: the right to be free from
governmental violation of the integrity of the individual (torture); the right to
the fulfillment of such vital needs as food, shelter, health care, and education; and the right to enjoy civil and political liberties. Despite the obvious
difficulty of translating general theory into uniform bureaucratic action, and
despite charges by Western European allies that the administration was
naive and formulated "policy from the pulpit," the president's advocacy of
human rights went a long way toward enhancing America's reputation as the
leading defender in this area. The administration's reasoning that the defense of basic human rights did not per se constitute interference in the internal affairs of other nations was probably too subtle for the Soviets, whose
own influential dissenters drew much inspiration and succor from
Washington. In any case, the policy fully distanced the Carter White House
from what had gone before.

In other areas, in Panama and China, President Carter built on the
firmer foundation of the Nixon and Ford policies. By 1974, the United
States and Panama had made much progress in the renegotiation of an
entirely new treaty respecting the Panama Canal Zone, agreeing in principle to the abrogation of the original treaty of 1903 and its amendments—
elimination of the concept of perpetuity, and the termination of U.S. jurisdiction over Panamanian territory. Carter was determined to complete the
task. After prolonged and intense debate throughout 1977, two new

treaties ultimately emerged. The first, the Panama Canal Treaty, gave to America the continued primary responsibility for the operation and defense of the Canal until the year 2000; the second, the Treaty Concerning the Permanent Neutrality and Operation of the Panama Canal, pledged Panama to maintain the permanent neutrality of the Canal, with the understanding that the United States reserved for itself the right to defend the Canal from external aggression as long as it was in operation. Both treaties passed in the Senate in 1978 by identical votes of 68–32, only one more vote than the two-thirds needed for ratification. Unknown to the president was the order of the Panamanian head of state Brigadier-General Omar Torrijos to the National Guard to attack and blow up the Canal if the Senate had rejected the agreement. All in all, the administration managed to retain adequate control of the operation of the vital waterway, reestablish good relations with Panama, and stop dead in their tracks the advance into Central America of those subversive groups who were using the issue of North American colonialism to gain a foothold in the region.

With regard to the thorny issues surrounding the formal recognition of the People's Republic of China (PRC) the president, led by his national security adviser, set out to resolve the problems of how best to effect the resumption of diplomatic relations with Peking without unduly undermining the stability of the Taiwan regime. Then, on the evening of December 15, 1978, Carter announced on national television that Washington and Peking had at last agreed to recognize each other and reestablish diplomatic relations. In return for placing relations with Peking on an official footing, the administration consented to break diplomatic relations with Taiwan, withdraw its remaining seven hundred troops from that island, and abrogate its 1954 defense treaty with Taipei. Failure to secure a pledge from the PRC not to use force in the ultimate reabsorption of Taiwan into China provided evidence enough of the Georgian's putative naivete for the president's growing chorus of mainly conservative critics.

In the Middle East, Carter mounted a major effort to bring about a comprehensive settlement of the problems left there since the Arab-Israeli War of 1973. The administration's three basic elements to the solution to the Middle East question included a firm commitment to complete peace in the area, the establishment of recognized borders, and a resolution of the Palestinian issue. Much to the dismay of the newly elected Israeli government (the right-wing Likud party, headed by Menachem Begin), Carter personally stressed the necessity of resolving the Palestinian question, i.e., finding a "homeland" for the Palestinians as opposed to creating a separate Palestinian state out of the occupied West Bank and Gaza Strip; specifically, he believed the Palestinians, numbering roughly four million souls throughout the Arab world, should be given a chance to shed their status as homeless refugees and partake in a peace settlement, including the possibility of an entity of some kind in association with Jordan, the recipient of the lion's share of the original Palestine Mandate. It was also hoped to bring all the concerned parties to Geneva where the USSR, co-chairman of the short-lived Geneva Peace Conference in the Middle East, would preside over "a just and lasting settlement of the Arab-Israeli conflict."

Little was accomplished until the spectacular diplomatic initiative of Egyptian President Anwar el-Sadat, desperate to preserve the political peace in his country. On November 19, 1977, President Sadat electrified the world when he traveled to Israel to put before the Israeli Parliament his own peace proposals; one month later, Begin reciprocated with a similar unprecedented visit to Egypt, bringing his own peace proposals. In reply to Egyptian demands for an unqualified withdrawal from Arab territories occupied during the 1967 Middle East War and the establishment of a Palestinian state carved out of the West Bank of the Jordan River and Gaza Strip, Begin offered the demilitarization of the Sinai, the gradual withdrawal of occupied territory, and limited self-rule for Palestinian Arabs on the West Bank and Gaza. By the end of January 1978, Cairo and Jerusalem had become deadlocked over an agreement of principles that would shape the still-hoped-for Geneva meeting.

Then, in an equally dramatic development, President Carter met with President Sadat and Prime Minister Begin from September 5–17, 1978, at his mountain retreat, Camp David, in order to compose their differences. The outcome, generally considered the most important foreign policy achievement of the Administration, resulted in two major agreements: a Framework for Peace in the Middle East, and a Framework for the Conclusion of a Peace Treaty between Egypt and Israel—the latter concluded in Washington on March 26, 1979. While the Camp David frameworks finally brought peace to Egypt and Israel, problems such as a definition of Palestinian autonomy in the West Bank, together with the accelerated establishment of Israeli settlements there, continued to bedevil the Middle East peace process.

The Arms Race

Despite campaign criticism of Republican preoccupation with the Soviet Union in general and arms controls in particular, the Carter administration found itself devoting equal time and energy to these same matters. Putatively "free of that inordinate fear of communism" that had informed the policies of past administrations, and interested in pushing strategic *limitation* talks into *reduction* talks, President Carter approached the Soviets with two arms control alternatives. The first was simply to ratify the Vladivostok guidelines worked out in the Ford administration, albeit with overall weapons limits about 10 percent below the previously accepted figures. The second alternative, which was regarded by some as the most revolutionary arms proposal since the beginning of the Cold War, required substantial overall reductions in armaments, thereby lessening the vulnerability of either nation to a first strike by the other; imposed stringent limits on qualitative improvements in weapons; and reduced the threat from those missiles of most concern, the very large Soviet intercontinental missiles and the proposed American MX (Missile Experimental).

The Kremlin replied immediately and negatively to the latter proposal. Further progress was complicated by the administration's decision to develop the cruise missile, cancel the strategic B-1 bomber, and allocate funds for a "neutron" bomb, an enhanced radiation weapon.

The SALT negotiations took two years. The treaty, among other things, provided for an equal overall limit on the number of strategic nuclear delivery vehicles; an equal limit of 1,320 on the total number of launchers of MIRV ballistic missiles and heavy bombers with long-range cruise missiles; and an equal limit of 820 on launchers of MIRV ICBMs. Put another way, SALT II, for the first time, placed equal ceilings on the strategic arsenals of both sides, ending a previous numerical balance in favor of the USSR, the principal criticism, while preserving American options to proceed with forces deemed necessary to maintain the strategic balance. The last-minute details were ironed out in June 1979 when Carter traveled to Vienna to meet with Soviet leader Leonid Brezhnev and to sign the agreement. They also worked out guidelines for what was to have been SALT III. Brezhnev's admonition that, "If we do not succeed, God will not forgive us," struck a particularly responsive chord in the president, who sent the treaty to the Senate for approval on June 22, 1979. But the times were against ratification.

For one thing, the Republicans decided to make a campaign issue of the treaty; for another, the Soviets, perhaps inadvertently, decided to help them. Soviet involvement in the dispute between Somalia and Ethiopia in the Horn of Africa and in the Vietnamese invasion of Kampuchea (Cambodia) led critics to question the worth of signing a treaty with the Kremlin at this or any other time. The "discovery" of a Soviet brigade of two to three thousand men, which was seen to be contributing to tensions in the Caribbean and

Central American regions, reinforced in others a tendency to link Soviet behavior with the passage of SALT II.

Whatever chance there was disappeared altogether after the Soviet invasion of Afghanistan in December 1979. The invasion gave rise to fears for the security of Pakistan and Iran. In the end President Carter, who viewed the invasion as a stepping stone to possible control over much of the world's oil supplies, reacted fiercely to the situation, pledging in his January 1980 State of the Union Message that, "An attempt by any outside force to gain control of the Persian Gulf region will be regarded as an assault on the vital interests of the United States of America, and such an assault will be repelled by any means necessary, including military force."

In addition to proclaiming the "Carter Doctrine," the president ordered a partial grain embargo of the USSR, halted exports, and led a worldwide call for a boycott of the summer Olympic Games scheduled to be held in Moscow—a tactic only partially successful, though the United States stayed home. At the same time President Carter announced that, because of the Soviet invasion, further Senate consideration of SALT II was to be deferred.

Publicly admitting that he misjudged Soviet intentions, Carter proposed a record-high peacetime military budget of $196.4 billion—a 14.6 percent hike over the previous year—with a "real" increase, after inflation, of 4.6 percent. More than half of the budget was earmarked for personnel and preparedness costs, with the remainder for the new MX land missile, cruise missiles to be launched from bombers, more navy ships, improved army tanks, marine equipment positioned in the Indian Ocean theater as part of the newly created Rapid Deployment Joint Task Force (RDJTF), and research on laser guns for space warfare. The Task Force, since renamed Intervention Force, made up of army, marine, navy, and air force units, was designed to project rapid and effective strength to any part of the world where it may be required.

Iran and the Hostage Crisis

The Iranian Revolution of January 1979 set in train a series of crises that would be the virtual undoing of the Carter administration. In late 1977, in a visit to Teheran, President Carter lauded the supreme leader of Iran, Shah Mohammed Reza Pahlevi, a "progressive" autocrat and ruler of the Peacock Throne, as one who had managed to maintain an oasis of stability in a region of trouble. The fact of the matter was that the Shah had been propped up by strong American support for more than twenty-five years since the CIA-staged coup in 1953 that restored the young monarch to his throne after he had been deposed by Prime Minister Mohammed Mossadegh, who had nationalized Western-owned oil fields.

Oil rich and preoccupied with military security, the Shah was allowed unlimited access to American arms. Force-marching his people in several decades through changes that in other similar societies had taken centuries brought intense resistance across the broad spectrum of Iranian society, from the westernized middle class to radical students to rightwing Islamic fundamentalists led by the Shi'a clergy, namely the mullahs and ayatollahs, all of whom were muffled by repressive police action. Under pressure from human rights advocates in the Carter administration, the Shah made one concession after another, reining in the dreaded secret police and allowing street demonstrations to take place unopposed. From that point onward the roof fell in on the Peacock Throne as the Shah fled from Teheran in January 1979, taking up refuge, consecutively, in Egypt, Morocco, the Bahamas, Mexico, and then Panama.

Meanwhile, the charismatic leader of the Islamic Revolution, the Ayatollah Ruhollah Khomeini, who had been in exile in Paris, returned to Iran and fairly soon established himself as the revolutionary leader of Islamic fundamentalists, ruthlessly pushing aside Marxists, liberals, or any other opponents to his regime. Khomeini made it clear, moreover, that he sought the return of the Shah "to Iran to stand trial in public, for 50 years of crimes against the Persian people." It thus became a matter of great moment when on October 22, 1979, President Carter admitted the Shah to the United States ostensibly for cancer treatment; torn between the prospect of rebuilding normal relations with the new Iran and under drumbeat pressure from the Shah's closest American friends, including former secretary of state Henry Kissinger and David Rockefeller, chairman of the Chase Manhattan Bank, host to Iranian assets, Carter gave in against his better judgment, admittedly based on official Iranian assurances that the American Embassy in Teheran would continue to be protected.

This was not the case. On November 4 Iranian militants—Islamic fundamentalists and anti-American factions united mainly in their opposition to what they perceived as the bourgeois, pro-Western government of Iranian Prime Minister Bazargan—seized the American Embassy and took sixty-six American hostages, demanding that the United States return the deposed Shah. (Thirteen hostages—five women and eight black men—were released two weeks later.) More than any other single event, the plight of the fifty-two hostages dominated the imagination of the national and international public until their release four hundred forty-four days later. In America it became, without question, *the* media spectacle of the last half of the twentieth century, with daily reminders from CBS's Walter Cronkite and other media personalities of how long the hostages had been held.

At first, Carter moved cautiously, ordering the halt of oil imports from Iran and freezing all Iranian assets in the United States. In retrospect, it is clear that plans for freeing the hostages obsessed the administration, opening the way for bizarre diplomatic contacts of all kinds with Iran. Though supporting their president for many months, Americans gradually were overwhelmed by a sense of collective impotence, stimulated each day by some new affront to a hostage or a new insult to the flag. Even Carter's decision to call off formal campaigning for the 1980 presidential election until the crisis was solved had little effect.

Finally, with all rational avenues closed—it was difficult to find anyone in Iran with whom to deal—the president reached for a military option. On April 24, 1980, Carter ordered into Iran a rescue team of six C-130 transports and eight RH-53D helicopter gunships from the aircraft carrier *Nimitz*, on patrol in the Arabian Sea, to effect the hostages' release. Equipment failure in three of the helicopters had already forced the chief executive to abort the mission, when two of the remaining aircraft collided on the ground following a refueling operation in a remote desert location in Iran, dubbed "Desert One." Early on the morning of April 25, the president candidly accepted responsibility for the failure of the mission and the loss of Secretary of State Vance, who resigned in protest of Carter's use of force. Vance was replaced by Senator Edward Muskie of Maine.

After much taunting of the administration and the death of the Shah in Cairo in July, Khomeini set down in September the conditions for the hostages' release: the return of the Shah's wealth, cancellation of American claims, unfreezing of Iranian assets in American banks, and a promise not to interfere in Iran's affairs. After 444 days in captivity, the hostages were finally freed on January 20, 1981, Inauguration Day, their release coming after weeks of round-the-clock negotiations between the United States and Algeria, selected by Iran to act as intermediary in exchanges concerning the hostages.

The relief to the national psyche was overwhelming, and no more so than to the Georgian in the White House: "It is impossible for me to put into words how much the hostages had come to mean to me, or how moved I was that morning to know they were coming home." Few failed to understand.

Suggested Readings

Baker, James T. *A Southern Baptist in the White House.* 1977.
Bell, Coral. *President Carter and Foreign Policy.* 1980.

Brzezinski, Zbigniew. *Power and Principle: Memoirs of the National Security Adviser, 1977–1981.* 1983.

Califano, Joseph A. Jr. *Governing America: An Insider's Report from the White House and Cabinet.* 1981.

Carter, Jimmy. *Why Not the Best.* 1975.

————— . *Keeping Faith: Memoirs of a President.* 1982.

Ford, Gerald. *A Time to Heal: The Autobiography of Gerald Ford.* 1979.

Mollenhoff, Clark R. *The President Who Failed: Carter Out of Control.* 1980.

Nessen, Ron. *It Sure Looks Different from the Inside.* 1978.

Powell, Jody. *The Other Side of the Story.* 1984.

Queen, Richard and Hass, Patricia. *Inside and Out: Hostage to Iran, Hostage to Myself.* 1981.

Reeves, Richard. *A Ford, Not a Lincoln.* 1975.

Rubin, Barry. *Paved with Good Intention: The American Experience and Iran.* 1981.

Salinger, Pierre. *America Held Hostage.* 1981.

Schram, Martin. *Running for President 1976.* 1977.

Shogan, Robert. *Promises to Keep: Carter's First Hundred Days in Office.* 1977.

Vance, Cyrus. *Hard Choices.* 1983.

Vestal, Bud. *Jerry Ford, Up Close: An Investigative Biography.* 1974.

7

Ronald Reagan and the Triumph of Conservatism

While enrolled Republicans accounted for only 27 percent of the American electorate—with Democrats at 42 percent and Independents at 30 percent—the GOP looked forward to the 1980 presidential elections with great expectations. In addition to the growing frustration of the Iranian hostage crisis, the Carter administration faced seemingly intractable economic problems. During the heat of the preconvention primaries, in the spring of 1980, inflation had leaped to 13.3 percent—the highest level since the Great Depression of the 1930s—while unemployment reached 8 percent of the work force. Record high interest rates and a stagnant economy rounded out a fairly dismal picture. And though few had a cure, most knew the cause. By July according to the Harris poll, 78 percent of Americans disapproved of Jimmy Carter's handling of foreign affairs; an even larger number, 83 percent, disagreed with his treatment of the economy.

It was in this atmosphere of confidence, then, that the Republican National Convention gathered in Detroit in July, and nominated Ronald Reagan. The second son of a hapless, alcoholic shoe salesman, Ronald Wilson Reagan was born on February 6, 1911, in Tampico, Illinois, but grew up in Dixon, Illinois, ninety-five miles west of Chicago, deep in the American heartland. Reagan's father was Irish-Catholic and his mother, Scottish-Protestant. A product of a Tom Sawyer boyhood (poor but wholesome), Reagan worked his way through Eureka College, a small Christian church college near Peoria, graduated in 1932 with a Bachelor of Arts degree in economics and sociology, and took up sportscasting. A job as a radio relay announcer for the Chicago Cubs games in Des Moines, Iowa, led him to California spring training camp, where he won a Warner Brothers screen test and launched his film career.

Beginning in 1937, Reagan was cast in fifty-five motion pictures, ranging from the memorable "Brother Rat" (1938), "Knute Rockne—All American" (1940), and "Kings Row" (1942), to the forgettable "Naughty But Nice" (1939), "John Loves Mary" (1949), and "Bedtime for Bonzo" (1951). Reagan's movie career plummeted in the 1950s, and after his discharge from the Army Air Corps Special Services, he immersed himself in the politics of the Screen Actors Guild, serving six terms as its president. Shifting easily to television, Reagan hosted the popular General Electric Theater; as spokesman for the company, he toured plants and lectured workers on the virtues of a free market economy and evils of Big Government, into the bargain converting from New Deal Democrat to conservative Republican.

Reagan's political career began in earnest in California with a surprise victory over incumbent Governor Edmund Brown in 1967, winning reelection in 1970. In 1968 the erstwhile movie star with the proverbial fire in the belly—a burning lust for high office—made his first bid for the Republican presidential nomination; in 1976 he came within sixty votes of wresting it from President Ford; in 1980 he swept all before him. The only real suspense at Detroit was the Californian's choice of a running mate. After an apparent overture to Gerald Ford, whose price for the proposed "dream ticket" proved too high, Reagan selected George Bush, an easterner and representative of the pragmatic conservative wing of the party, as well as the last challenger in the presidential primaries. Chosen for considerations of geographical balance and experience, Bush had served as a former congressman, chief delegate to the United Nations, and director of the Central Intelligence Agency.

"As your nominee," declared the sixty-nine year old Reagan to the party faithful in his acceptance speech, "I pledge to restore to the Federal government the capacity to do the people's work without dominating their lives. I pledge to you a government that will not only work well, but wisely; its ability to act tempered by prudence, and its willingness to do good balanced by the knowledge that government is never more dangerous than when our desire to have it help us blinds us to its great power to harm us." Invoking the spirit if not the works of Franklin Delano Roosevelt—a classic example of divorcing words from their meanings—Reagan proposed to revive the economy by cutting taxes (a 30 percent reduction in income tax rates over a period of three years), and by cutting Federal budgets while vastly increasing defense spending, all of which was supposed to be accomplished by the application of the theory of "supply-side economics."

According to Reagan, who had borrowed the concept from economist Arthur Laffer who, for his part, had borrowed it from nineteenth-century French economist Jean Baptiste Say, sharp tax cuts would stimulate the economy sufficiently to yield a recovery strong enough to compensate for lost revenue while wiping out the Federal deficit. Put another way, supply rather than scarcity would increase demand. A simpler, less painless remedy for the recession could not be imagined. On other specific issues, the GOP party platform opposed the "windfall Profits tax" and the peacetime draft; pledged to nominate a woman to the Supreme Court; supported a constitutional ban on court-ordered busing as a "last resort," as well as a similar ban on all abortions except those needed to save a woman's life; supported equal rights for women at the same time opposing the Equal Rights Amendment; vowed to replace detailed (restrictive) environmental rules with more flexible standards; proposed giving states and localities greater control over general programs along with Federal block grants to pay for benefits.

Embattled, embittered, and more than a little apprehensive of their chances in the fall, delegates to the Democratic National Convention, meeting again in New York in August, renominated President Carter on the first ballot. Throughout the primaries, up to a victory on a key vote on rules in the opening session of the convention, Carter managed to contain the challenge of Senator Edward Kennedy of Massachusetts whose own drive for the presidential nomination seemed long on promise but short on performance, with the notable exception of the senator's emotional address to the delegates attacking Ronald Reagan's "voyage into the past." The president's acceptance speech, marking the start of an uphill battle against his Republican rival, sought to make Ronald Reagan himself the major issue in the campaign. "The choice—the choice between the two paths to the future—could not be more clear," the Georgian intoned. "If we succumb to a world of fantasy, we will wake up to a nightmare. But if we start with reality and fight to make our dreams a reality, all Americans will have a good life, a life of meaning and purpose as a nation strong and secure."

For others, the choice was more apparent than real. While the popular complaint was that the American people were once again being forced to choose between "the lesser of two evils," columnist James Reston of the *New York Times* complained that the problem was really "the evils of two lessers." Even for some of the president's supporters, it was no more than an "unhappy choice." To journalist Garry Wills, Reagan was "so patently unmalicious as he speaks for war and divisiveness that he may, indeed, kill us with kindness . . . the wholesome hometown sort who can drop the bomb without a second thought, your basic American Harry Truman." A former governor, generally unexperienced in foreign affairs and an outsider in Washington, Reagan could only run on the promise that he could do the job better.

Among the more significant aspects of the 1980 presidential election was the alternative candidacy of John B. Anderson, the twenty-year liberal Republican congressman from Illinois, whose ratings in the polls ranged from a high of 20 to 25 percent in the summer to less than 15 percent in September. The chief beneficiary of discontent among the electorate with the direction of the country and the weakness of the party system, Anderson advocated a 50-cents-a-gallon gasoline tax to enforce conservation, the ratification of SALT II and ERA, and approved enforcement of civil rights laws. With little organization and even fewer funds, Anderson had to content himself with focusing on the major problems on the national agenda while the two principal candidates focused on each other, though the Democrats fretted with the prospect of a vote for Anderson amounting to a vote for Reagan.

The other major feature of an otherwise uneventful campaign was the last-minute television debate between Carter and Reagan in Cleveland in late October, under the auspices of the League of Women Voters. For ninety minutes Reagan, appearing calm and reasonable, and Carter, appearing unusually stiff and wooden—in any case a far cry from presidential—slogged through a litany of where each stood on the issues and where his rival erred. The debate, watched by a television audience of sixty to one hundred million viewers, was perhaps the most important event of the long campaign, while at stake were the opinions of virtually millions of yet undecided voters in key states whose electoral votes would determine the outcome.

Who won the debate? According to one analyst, "There was no winner—only survivors. The voters lost." The *New York Times* remarked editorially, "Mr. Reagan is a better salesman but the president, though he keeps dropping the sample case on his own foot, offers better goods." What was astonishing was that Jimmy Carter, saddled with the highest inflation rate since World War II and the Iranian hostage crisis, was still in the race. With just a week to go, the president had managed to wipe out his opponent's seemingly unassailable lead of the summer. In fact, on the eve of the voting, the election appeared "too close to call." What happened next surprised everybody, including the pundits: Reagan won easily, with a margin of about 10 percent in the popular vote 42,951,045 (51 percent) to 34,600,037 (41 percent) and a margin of 440 electoral votes (489 to 49). Carter became the first elected incumbent president to be defeated in a bid for reelection since Herbert Hoover in 1932.

Significantly, the Republicans wrested control of the Senate for the first time since 1952 (53–46, plus 1 independent), turning out such well-known liberals as Senators George McGovern (Democrat, South Dakota) and Frank Church (Democrat, Idaho). The Reagan-led counterrevolution also substantially reduced the Democratic majority in the House of Representatives (242–192, with 1 independent). And for the first time since World War I, the two houses were controlled by different parties, there having been a Democratic majority in both houses since 1955.

The so-called Reagan Revolution owed much to Ronald Reagan's appeal to traditional Democrats, particularly blue-collar workers, often urban Catholics from the Northeast and Middle West, and southern Protestants, often rural and religious, who had been Democrats since the Civil War. Bringing the traditional party of the country club and the boardroom into the bowling alley and the union hall, while promising to fight crime, end racial disruptions in the schools, cut taxes, shore up the family, and, rationalize welfare, required the special talent of the "Great Communicator"—and a lot of money.

Electing the president and winning control of the Senate cost the GOP $170 million, five times as much as the Democrats, who spent only $35 million on their own campaigns. Finally, one may attribute the Republican success in 1980 to the widely held view that the average American voter—and only 52.3 percent of the electorate eligible to vote cast their ballots, marking twenty years of a progressive decline in voter turnout—had had enough of Jimmy Carter and the period of national self-questioning with which the Georgian was readily identified.

To Dream Heroic Dreams

The first certified conservative to enter the White House in more than fifty years, the fortieth president promised, before all else, to "Get the Government off the backs of the people." Or, as he put it in his inaugural speech (judged a theatrical triumph): "In this present crisis, government is not the solution to our problem; government is the problem." To make his point, only minutes after completing his speech, Reagan ordered a freeze on the hiring of civilian employees by all executive departments and agencies of the

Federal government—the opening act of a political conservative reformation that aimed at nothing less than the reversal of the liberal New Deal revolution of governmental activism and Democratic party dominance established by Franklin Roosevelt during the Great Depression.

Hoping to unleash the private sector whose instincts, according to Democrats, could not be trusted to produce progress and social justice without the oversight of government, Reagan called upon the creative energy of the American people to "begin an era of national renewal":

Let us renew our determination, our courage and our strength. And let us renew our faith and hope. We have every right to dream heroic dreams.

Those who say that we're in a time when there are no heroes—they just don't know where to look.

Few could doubt the president had the gift of speech. Translating the "new beginning" into policy would be something else again.

To get from here to there, Reagan filled his administration with (in his words), "people who don't want a job in Government. I want people who are already so successful that they would regard a Government job as a step down, not a step up." Most typical of this kind of thinking was the appointment of Donald T. Regan, chairman of the stock brokerage giant, Merrill Lynch, as secretary of the treasury; Casper V. Weinberger, vice-president and director of the Bechtel Power Corporation, as secretary of defense; and Samuel R. Pierce, Jr., a black man who was then senior partner in one of New York's major law firms, as secretary of housing and urban development. Less typical was the appointment of retired army general and former Supreme Allied Commander in Europe, Alexander M. Haig, Jr., as secretary of state; Richard V. Allen, campaign adviser on foreign policy, as assistant for national security affairs; and David A. Stockman, a young conservative in a hurry, as director of the Office of Management and Budget. (Haig and Allen, for various reasons, were replaced, respectively, by George P. Schultz, an academic and economist also from the Bechtel Corporation, and William Clark from California, Reagan's political crony whose lack of knowledge about world leaders became the stuff of comedy. Prominent women in the cabinet included Jeanne J. Kirkpatrick, a conservative Democrat and political scientist who became U.S. ambassador to the United Nations; Elizabeth Dole (wife of Senator Robert Dole) who became secretary of health and human services; and Margaret M. Heckler, a former congresswoman from Massachusetts who became secretary of transportation.

Without doubt, the most controversial of the appointments was that of

Denver attorney James G. Watt, an ultraconservative and a born-again Christian, to head the Department of the Interior. In the face of strident opposition from environmentalists and conservationists, who had fought for years to keep undeveloped regions in something akin to their natural state, Watt led the most sweeping and controversial drive in the nation's history to convert Federal lands to commercial use and defied congressional critics in his efforts, largely successful, to open huge stretches of the Atlantic and Pacific coasts to offshore oil and gas drilling. All the while, he barred new additions to the wilderness system. In October 1983, the embattled secretary of the interior was forced from his post for referring to the Coal-Leasing Commission as "a black, a woman, two Jews and a cripple." For Watt's place the president then proposed National Security Adviser "Bill" Clark who, according to Reagan, was "a God-fearing westerner, a fourth-generation rancher, and a person I trust."

Less controversial was the nomination in July 1981 of the first woman in the nation's history to serve on the Supreme Court, Judge Sandra O'Connor, of the Arizona Court of Appeals. Within a short time she forged a close alliance with the Supreme Court's two leading conservatives, Chief Justice Warren E. Burger and Associate Justice William H. Rehnquist, providing a needed vote on issues ranging from criminal laws to presidential immunity. For middle-level appointments in subcabinet offices, independent agencies and independent regulatory commissions, the administration turned increasingly to people whose lack of experience in, and hostility to, Federal government were deemed, it seemed, sole qualifications for their posts. Not surprisingly, a number of the inexperienced brought more than the usual embarrassment: an assistant secretary of Housing and Urban Development was suspended after allegations that he had used his staff to prepare a personal manuscript for publication; the chief of the Veteran's Administration resigned after it was learned that he had retained his chauffeur for personal use and spent $54,000 to redecorate his office; and several appointees at the Legal Services Corporation were dismissed when it was disclosed they had arranged exorbitant consulting fees while attempting to curb legal aid for the poor.

The very tone of the Reagan presidency differed sharply from that of its predecessor. "This is a fun administration," commented a member of the Presidential Inaugural Committee, referring to the conspicuous spending habits of the more visible members of the Reagan White House. Charles Z. Wick, director of the U.S. Information Agency (who, in addition to belonging to the president's "kitchen cabinet" of California business executives, wrote and produced the film "Snow White and the Three Stooges"), suggested that economically pinched Americans of today would probably enjoy viewing the luxurious Washington way of life of the Reagan administration players, as much as Americans who suffered during the Great Depression enjoyed watching Hollywood stars in the movies. At that time Americans down on their luck would go to the movies because, "They loved those glamorous pictures showing people driving beautiful cars and women in beautiful gowns, showing that people were living the glamorous good life." (The president's wife Nancy, a former starlet, arrived in Washington with an inaugural wardrobe estimated at $25,000.)

The president's personal philosophy of government generally reflected the views of his closest friends, mainly self-made millionaires, who had followed the American Dream to its logical conclusion. "Running the government is like running General Motors," explained a Reagan confidant, the late, controversial Alfred S. Bloomingdale, former board chairman of the Diner's Club. "It's twice General Motors or three times General Motors—but it's General Motors." Skeptics of the strictly business approach to the government of the United States remained unconvinced.

Toward the New Federalism

In its two years, which ended just before the closing days of 1982, the 97th Congress implemented more tax changes than any other Congress. During the first half of the two-year session, Congress under the lash of Reaganomics approved the largest tax cut in American history, an estimated $750 billion over five years. Skillfully utilizing the wave of sympathy that followed an assassination attempt on his life in late March by John W. Hinckley, an enigmatic, twenty-five-year-old, well-off dropout (subsequently found not guilty due to insanity), the president persuaded lawmakers to pass 90 percent of his economic program, comprising "a new beginning." In addition to slashing nearly $140 billion in funding for Federal programs over a three-year period, administration accomplishments included, among other things, a 25 percent cut in individual income tax over three years, with a provision to index taxes to changes in the Consumer Price Index (to begin in 1985); a lowering to 50 percent of the maximum tax on investment income; a raising of the estate exemption and gift exclusion taxes; an increase in the exemption of the windfall-profits tax on oil producers; faster depreciation of investments by businesses; and tax relief for small businesses and corporations. The object of the exercise, reversing a fifty-year tide of increased government spending, was supposed to result in a surge of productivity that would ultimately lead to increased Federal revenues and lower interest rates and inflation.

As it turned out, supply-side economics had only a few of the answers. Inflation was cut from 12 percent when Reagan took office to 3.9 percent in 1982, the smallest rate of inflation since 1972 when price controls were in effect; similarly, interest rates declined from 21.5 percent to 11.5 percent at the end of 1982. That was the good news.

The bad news was the severe recession that accompanied the dramatic reduction in the underlying rate of inflation. In spite of—some said because of—Reaganomics, the economy witnessed a sharp real decline of 5 percent in Gross National Product, the goods and services produced by the nation and the broadest gauge of economic health, while unemployment reached a forty-two year high of 10.4 percent, with 11.5 million people officially unemployed; at times during 1982 a record 22 percent of the labor force was unemployed. States such as Michigan, with its heavy concentration of automobile manufacturing, reached well above that mark, while white (20.8 percent) and black teenagers (48.1 percent) were the hardest hit. An estimated 225,000 to 3 million people were living in the streets of America, and one in seven Americans—nearly 32 million—were living below the official poverty line, the highest increase since the days of Lyndon Johnson's war on poverty. Joblessness, according to a Gallup poll taken in 1982, had replaced inflation as the number one concern of Americans.

The problem was generally attributed to a Federal budget that remained wildly out of balance, with projections of record deficits exceeding $150 billion a year. Put another way, the budget deficits maintained by heavy borrowing from abroad continually threatened to raise inflationary expectations and interest rates, still considered too high, choking off recovery.

The president responded in two ways. First, in August 1982, he proposed further cuts of $30 billion over a three-year period from Federal programs, including food stamps, Medicare, Medicaid, and pensions. Second, and swallowing hard, Reagan pushed through the same 97th Congress the largest revenue-raising package in history, suggesting that his support of a tax increase in no way represented "any reversal of policy or philosophy" but rather a mid-course correction. Designed to raise $98.3 billion in three years, the measure sought, among other things, to close off special-interest loopholes, enforce stricter compliance of current tax laws and increase excise taxes on cigarettes, telephone service, and airline tickets. Supported by a collection of strange bedfellows, ranging from liberal Democrats such as Senator Edward Kennedy (Democrat, Massachusetts) to the more conservative Robert Dole (Republican, Kansas), the bill passed by a margin of 226 to 107 in the House and 52 to 47 in the Senate.

Advocates of supply-side economics, including New Right Republicans who broke ranks with the White House, were furious. "This is not the same man we elected," lamented the high priest of the theory, Arthur Laffer. "This tax package is obnoxious." In fact, supply-siders, none of whom, incidentally, had been appointed to the White House staff, were able to keep the president on course for only his first year in office; since that time, critics argued, the advisers with the readiest access to Reagan were mainly those who saw tax increases as the means to a stronger economy.

In other notable legislation the 97th Congress made considerable headway. It passed the Voting Rights Act of 1982, extending basic provisions of the voting laws of 1965, 1970, and 1975; a Veteran's Bill providing cost-of-living benefit increases averaging 11.2 percent to 2.3 million service-disabled veterans and their survivors; a 5-cent-a-gallon increase in the gasoline tax to finance highway repairs and mass transit; and historic legislation setting a timetable and procedure for creating a permanent burial site for radioactive waste, which had been accumulating since World War II.

On his own, the president formally introduced proceedings to disband the Department of Energy, in line with his election promise, and freed oil companies from regulations limiting the amount of lead in petroleum products. Reagan also announced a government-farmer "crop swap" to curb grain production in an effort to relieve economic distress in the nation's farms whose net income had fallen in 1982 to the lowest point since 1933; under the program, the Department of Agriculture would "pay" farmers from stored grain surpluses to hold down their plantings, the aim being to remove 23 million acres of wheat, corn, rice, and sorghum from production.

In the mid-term elections in November, the administration lost twenty-six seats in the House of Representatives, fully twice as many as it expected to lose. At the very least, the Democrats who had momentarily recaptured the image as the party best able to ensure the nation's prosperity (according to the Gallup poll), threatened the ideological majority Reagan had forged to push through so many of his economic proposals during the first half of his term in the White House. The Republicans, however, managed to retain their eight-seat majority in the Senate, each side having made two gains there. Reagan, the first GOP president since Eisenhower to work with a Senate controlled by members of his own party, could once again look forward to the cooperation of the upper chamber. Republican losses arose largely from popular dissatisfaction with Reaganomics, with its association, deserved or not, of unconcern for the needy. The fact that in 1982 Republicans were most popular with white males earning more than $40,000 a year was not lost even on Republicans concerned with widening the party's grass roots appeal.

The president's earlier political magic faded, however, as the 98th Congress repeatedly defied Reagan on economic and military issues. A proposed overhaul of the immigration laws languished in a House-Senate conference, a major civil rights bill overwhelmingly approved by the House was killed in the Senate, and a banking deregulation bill that the Senate approved died in a House committee. Unlike its predecessor, which gave the president the spending, tax, and military bills he sought, the 98th Congress balked at further cuts on social spending and reduced by more than half the increase he sought for the military. It approved $249 billion for fiscal year 1984, rejecting along the way nerve gas weapons but approving funds for twenty-one MX missiles, B-1 long-range bombers, and testing of antisubmarine weapons. Congress finally approved the Caribbean Basin initiative providing trade and tax benefits to poorer Caribbean nations. In the case of Nicaragua, Congress approved $24 million in covert aid to rebels, while in El Salvador, it made additional funds contingent on land reforms and improvements in the criminal justice system.

The 98th Congress worked well in other areas. Through a bipartisan commission appointed by President Reagan, a revision of the Social Security system was finally approved, requiring new Federal employees and employees of nonprofit organizations to join the system, new payroll tax increases, a tax on benefits paid to more affluent retired persons, and a rise in the retirement age by two years (to 67 years old by the year 2027). In the sensitive area of abortion, Congress expanded its ban on using Federal funds for abortions by prohibiting such use by Federal employees' health plans. Congress also approved the program initiated by the president to give farmers government-owned commodities in return for curtailed production of surplus crops—the swap-crop plan. Another bill for the first time would pay dairy farmers for reducing their milk production. Transcending partisanship, the majority of congressmen approved legislation for a Federal holiday on the birthday of the Reverend Dr. Martin Luther King, Jr. Congress also repealed the 10 percent withholding tax on interest and dividends scheduled to have taken effect on July 1.

President Reagan held that the single greatest failure of the 98th Congress was its inability to pass a responsible budget to help bring down deficits. "By responsible," he said, "I do not mean a budget that reduces spending to match revenues." Lawmakers, on the other hand, replied that the one major reason for the deficit was the president's adamant insistence on higher military spending and lower taxes. Congress itself was reluctant to close the gap until the administration took the lead and provided political cover for unpopular decisions that would eventually be required.

During the 1980 presidential campaign, Reagan indicated that he wished to move beyond President Nixon's concept of revenue sharing, which accounted for the distribution of $64.9 billion in Federal tax revenue to state and local governments since 1972, to a "new federalism":

Basically, I want to change the course we've been on in which Washington was seen as the answer to all the problems. I want to restore the balance between the different levels of government that has been so distorted in recent decades . . . to restore functions that properly belong at different levels of government to those levels; and to restore also the taxing power that has been pre-empted, turn much of it back to local government and state government.

Under the initial "new federalism," outlined by the president in his January 1982 State of the Union Message, the Federal government would assume full responsibility for medical aid to the poor, and the states, in turn, would assume responsibility for the food stamp program and aid to families with dependent children—the principal programs of cash assistance to the poor. In addition, more than forty education, transportation, and social service programs would be taken over by the states, along with some money to pay for them. The plan's simplicity, argued critics, masked its very radicalism, for it sought nothing less than to reverse the powerful centralizing trend in American public life that dates from the beginning of the century. Under the administration proposal, a Federal trust fund would help finance the program taken over by the states from 1984 through 1991; after that, the fund would disappear and the states could raise or lower taxes as they saw fit.

The states, already economically strapped, entertained serious doubts about the economic viability of the proposal. And as opposition mounted, the White House revised the plan, reducing the list of programs transferred while retaining the food stamp program. By the end of 1982, this particular plan was dead. The idea had died, according to one influential state governor, because it was not really a sorting out of programs among Federal and state governments, but rather a shift to states, cities, and counties of problems that were beyond their ability to handle. A much watered-down version of the president's "new federalism" plan, turning over even fewer programs to the states while promising them a stable level of funding for five years, was submitted to Congress with small hope of passage. (The 1986 Federal budget, worked out in the summer of 1985, proposed killing revenue sharing in 1987.)

A Counterrevolution in Civil Rights

Buttressed by arguments of free-market economists with good White House connections and generally antipathetical to Federal activism, President Reagan entered office adamantly opposed to busing and job quotas. As a matter of philosophy, if not necessarily of action, the administration had reversed President Carter's support of mandatory busing as a means of desegregating the nation's school systems, calling it ineffective and instead promoting voluntary transfers. The president, by all accounts a decent and honest man without an apparent racist bone in his body, adhered to the belief that court-ordered busing could itself be a "violation of the rights of the community," adding that the people who were supposed to benefit most, the black community, were doing much of the protesting.

Forced busing, as a permanent solution to the problem of how to integrate society, was perceived by some as discriminatory to blacks themselves because it was mainly the minority student who was being asked to quit his neighborhood early each morning often with questionable results. "As a black person and as an American," commented a leading exponent of black conservative views, economist Walter F. William, "I'm for high-quality education. But it is not clear to me that to get (it), black people have to go out and capture a white kid for their children to sit beside." Others, equally representative of the nation's 26.5 million blacks—11.7 percent of a total population of 226.5 million—regarded such attitudes as borne of frustration and regretted that the administration had elected to raise an issue that was thought settled by the Supreme Court in 1954. Experience, according to the Reagan Justice Department, had instead shown court-ordered busing to be a failed experiment.

The White House was no less relenting in the matter of job quotas; Reagan made it clear that he would no longer insist that employers found guilty of sexual or racial discrimination abide by quotas in their future job-hiring promises. Specifically, noted the chief of the Justice Department's civil rights division, the administration would "no longer insist upon or in any respect support the use of quotas or any other numerical or statistical formulas designed to provide nonvictims of discrimination preferential treatment based on race, sex, national origin or religion." In the future, remedy would only be available to individual members of minority groups who could demonstrate that they had personally been the victims of discrimination. Race-conscious or sex-conscious preferences had, according to this logic, proved historically divisive, well beyond the remedy that was necessary to redress the injured party. Blacks and their liberal allies, looking through the tangle of interpretations that had been placed between them and the customary statutory redress they had come to count upon, found cold comfort in this Republican administration, affording Reagan little political support which he repaid with only a handful of Federal appointments.

Revitalizing Containment

Not unlike his Republican predecessor in the Oval Office, Richard Nixon, President Ronald Reagan made the management of the Soviet-American relationship the centerpiece of his administration's foreign policy; unlike Nixon, however, he had no faith in the ability of the Kremlin to behave properly. How does one conduct business, the president reasoned publicly, with leaders who reserve "unto themselves the right to commit any crime, to lie, to cheat," all in the name of world revolution? How does one deal with leaders who "don't subscribe to our idea of morality, who don't believe in an afterlife, who don't believe in God or a religion?"

Perceiving the Soviet Union as dangerous, expansionary, and antagonistic to American interests everywhere, the administration, led by Secretary of Defense Caspar Weinberger and Secretary of State Alexander Haig, argued that the only way to deal with the threat was to maintain a much stronger military establishment, beginning with a restoration of the margin of nuclear superiority or safety purportedly lost by Jimmy Carter. To meet what Haig identified as "the most complete reversal of global power relationships ever seen in a period of relative peace," the administration further urged a broad-based, unilateral defense buildup, a strengthening of allied ties and a return to a policy of containing Soviet power and influence—in short, to revitalizing the policy of containment, though just what this meant was never quite clear. As for pursuing the expansion of human rights, the Reagan White House served notice that it had no intention of preaching American ideals to other friendly countries, especially those in Central and Latin America. The world was judged too dangerous a place to do otherwise.

In 1981 the administration committed a staggering $1.5 trillion over the next five years to the largest peacetime military buildup in the nation's history, paying special attention to the modernization of the strategic nuclear forces in order to be in a position of strength at the negotiating table. Specifically, the White House increased defense spending from 1981 to 1982 by 20 percent, to $211 billion, and from 1982 to 1983 by 14 percent, to $241 billion; the requests for 1984 and 1985 were on the order of $245 billion and $277 billion, respectively.

Reagan swept into office, then, committed to the notion of restoring America's presumed margin of nuclear safety (actually, superiority), in the process closing the nation's "window of vulnerability"—that much-talked-about potential in the near future of the Soviet Union taking out the country's ICBM force with enough in reserve to cause the president to hesitate in launching a second strike. The president's supporters, who have remained persuaded beyond doubt that the Soviet Union today constitutes a threat of direct miliary action of unprecedented proportions, have not been disappointed. Reagan proceeded apace with the B-1 strategic bombers (which Carter had cancelled), nuclear submarines, Trident submarine-launched missiles, the MX (though basing and quantity still pose a problem), and the neutron bomb, an enhanced radiation weapon that spews lethal neutrons out beyond the range of blast and heat, killing or injuring all living matter in its wake but leaving nonliving matter untouched—the quintessential antipersonnel weapon.

This was all too much for the growing and influential antinuclear movement that began first in Europe and spread to the United States. It was only a matter of time before even Reagan would have to react to "thinking the unthinkable"—thinking aloud about waging and winning a limited controlled nuclear war and nuclear "warning shots." And react he did. In November 1981 the president proposed a "Zero Option" for intermediate-range nuclear arms in Europe under which Washington and NATO would cancel deployment of Pershing II and ground-launched cruise missiles if Moscow would dismantle its own SS-20, SS-4 and SS-5 missles.

More significantly, on May 9, 1982, on the occasion of a commencement address at his alma mater, Eureka College in Illinois, Reagan issued a call for what he termed Strategic Arms Reduction Talks (START), proposing in the first phase a one-third cut in strategic warheads, a ceiling of no more than one-half of the remaining strategic warheads to be placed on land-based missiles, and a reduction of the total number of ballistic missiles to an equal level of about one-half the current U.S. level. In June 1983 Reagan slightly revised the START offer, making the minimum necessary changes in his negotiating approach to capture a congressional majority for the limited production of the MX missile but not enough to reach a breakthrough with the Soviets in Geneva. In order to make room for a new, small, compromise missile with a single warhead—the Midgetman—Reagan raised the proposed ceiling of long-range ballistic missiles on each side from 850 to 1,200. The Kremlin's counterproposal called for a ceiling of 1,800 missiles and long-range bombers for each side, of which 1,450 would be missiles. The "gap" was thus closed to 250. Presently the United States had approximately 1,600 such missiles and the Soviets 2,350. Talks on both issues, broken off by the Soviets in November 1983, were once again underway in Geneva. The outcome may require years of bargaining.

Critics disagreed with the administration's view that many of President Reagan's proposals were plainly and sensibly aimed at arms control, so long as the principal objective of the exercise was to lessen the likelihood of *anyone* starting a nuclear war. This administration had, in their judgment, moved further and further away from the traditional doctrine of retaliation, to the doctrine of nuclear war fighting. Even moderates were disturbed to learn of the growing belief in the Pentagon that the only way to deter the Kremlin was to show it that America, too, was capable of waging and winning a nuclear war, preferring arms control agreements that returned to MAD and, presumably, to stability.

What the administration should have done, according to this line of reasoning, was swallowed hard and pushed the SALT II Treaty, warts and all, through the Senate, instead of complaining that the Soviets were in violation of it. In addition the president could also have used his influence in the Senate to push along the Threshold Test Ban Treaty, as well as the Treaty on Underground Nuclear Explosion for Peaceful Purposes, both of which were still, physically and legally, before the Senate. In the judgment of some, Reagan could have had it both ways: modernization of the nation's nuclear force structure though perhaps more gradually, and a reputation as a "peacemaker." Strategically, this means, to paraphrase former CIA director Stanfield Turner, recommitting the nation to a nuclear doctrine of assured retaliation.

As the United States and the Soviet Union moved into the mid-1980s, the fourth decade of nuclear rivalry, their adversarial relationship remained essentially unchanged. Each nation was still beset with fears and suspicions of the other. They were still, in the famous image of atomic scientist Robert Oppenheimer, like two scorpions in a bottle, compelled by self-preservation to match their adversary's every move. To date, the arms control movement has only had limited success in reducing such fears and in restraining nuclear innovations of a threatening kind.

The principal challenge facing the superpowers in the remainder of this century was to devise a diplomatic solution in which arms control could, at long last, overtake the arms race. Finally, there also had to be developed a strategy to persuade the public and politicians alike that despite the notion of "margin of safety," which doubtless appealed to elements on both sides of the Iron Curtain, that in an open-ended arms race, by which there is a determination to match system for system, there was only losing for those who could think of nothing but winning.

It is in this sense that President Reagan's recent preoccupation with a Star Wars version of a space-based antiballistic missile system, replacing thermonuclear weapons designed to kill people with energy-directed weapons designed to kill other weapons, was a step in the wrong direction in that it threatened to undermine one of the few notable achievements of arms control—the ABM Treaty of 1972—while launching the superpowers into a runaway race in offensive *and* defensive weapons. Perhaps someday each side will find the political will to solve the nuclear question, but until then we shall have to keep our faith in what Winston Churchill once called the "process of sublime irony," whereby safety continues to remain "the sturdy child of terror, and survival the twin brother of annihilation."

In other crisis areas overseas—Afghanistan, Poland, and Lebanon—the administration responded with considerable restraint. While stressing the desirability of an acceptable political solution to the withdrawal of Soviet occupation forces in Afghanistan, the president, true to his election promise, lifted the partial grain embargo on the USSR in April 1981. During the campaign, Reagan had called the embargo ineffective and an unfair burden on the American farmer. In Poland where the independent trade union movement, Solidarity, was crushed by martial law in December 1981, the administration imposed various economic sanctions, including the suspension of special trade status for Warsaw, in retaliation for continued repression by that country's Soviet-backed military regime. The White House, together with the NATO allies, warned the Soviet Union in particular that intervention in Poland would fundamentally alter the entire international situation and effectively destroy prospects of workable East-West relations.

Persuaded that the Kremlin was deliberately using the crisis to sow dissension within the West, Reagan, encouraged by Secretary Haig, imposed additional economic sanctions against the Soviet Union, principally by reducing exports of advanced technology to prompt Moscow to back down on Poland. None of these measures, including a failed, heavy-handed effort to curb European participation on the Siberian gas export pipeline, had much apparent success.

And finally, in the Middle East, the administration, with the dogged determination of American Ambassador Philip Habib, ended the hostilities that had culminated in the summer of 1982 when Israelis invaded southern Lebanon and Beirut to eliminate the threat posed by large numbers of Palestinian Liberation Organization (PLO) fighters. Shortly afterward, Habib negotiated the evacuation of the PLO and the Syrians from West Beirut; the Syrians had been deeply involved in the Lebanese Civil War since 1976. In August and again in October, following the assassination of the newly elected Lebanese president and the massacre of Palestinian civilians in their refugee camps, President Reagan sent American troops to join a multinational force to help the new government there begin efforts to restore its authority throughout the war-torn country.

On the successful evacuation from Beirut, the president urged what he called a "fresh start" in Middle East peace negotiations, building on the Camp David accords worked out in the Carter presidency. Specifically, he outlined a policy of self-government by the Palestinians of the West Bank and Gaza in association with the state of Jordan; a settlement freeze by Israel; guarantees of the security of Israel; and an undivided Jerusalem, with its final status to be decided through negotiation. Reagan, together with new Secretary of State George Schultz, who had replaced Haig at the height of the Israeli invasion, received little support for his efforts. Both Israel and the PLO, each for its own reasons, rejected the proposal. Nevertheless, Reagan regarded the Middle East initiative as "probably the greatest" foreign policy accomplishment of his administration.

Within a year American policy in the region collapsed. In October 1983 suicide terrorists—most likely agents of Syria and Iran—driving bomb-laden trucks, blew up a United States Marine headquarters building in Beirut, resulting in the deaths of 241 Americans; after four months of domestic pressure and in view of the worsening situation in the Lebanese capital, the White House ordered the redeployment of marines from Beirut to warships offshore.

Domino Theory Revisited

From the first days of the administration, Secretary of State Haig was uneasy about Central America, particularly El Salvador, the smallest and most densely populated country in the region. Relentlessly, though with scanty proof, Haig mounted a major campaign around the world to draw attention to what he regarded as a "textbook case" of indirect armed aggression directed by communist powers through Cuba. In this instance, a leftist armed rebellion of about seven thousand guerillas in El Salvador was being supplied by way of Nicaragua, the largest and most sparsely populated country in Central America, under the control of the Marxist-dominated *Sandinistas* who in 1979 overthrew the hated right-wing dynasty established by Anastasio Somoza in 1936. The administration had no doubt that Nicaragua was the main support and command base for the Salvadoran guerillas, as well as leftist extremists in Guatemala, Honduras, and Costa Rica.

The situation in El Salvador, according to Haig, presented a strikingly familiar case of Soviet, Cuban, and other communist military involvement in a politically troubled Third World country. By providing arms, training, and direction to a local insurgency and by supporting it with a global propaganda campaign, the communists sought to intensify and widen the conflict, deceiving much of the world about the true nature of the revolution. The communist objective, the former NATO general continued, was to bring about—at little cost to themselves—the overthrow of the established government and the imposition of a regime in defiance of the will of the Salvadoran people. Time was of the essence. Haig, testifying before the House Foreign Affairs Committee in mid-March 1981, asserted that El Salvador was the latest on "a priority target list—a hit list, if you will, for the ultimate [Soviet] takeover of Central America."

The stage having thus been set, Haig advocated exerting maximum political, economic, and military pressure in 1981 to treat the problem at its source—Cuba—in effect "to force the issue early" in El Salvador, even if it brought a Soviet response. We now know from Haig's memoirs that his call for action found no support from the highest councilors of the White House who feared "another Vietnam" that in turn would sap public support for the administration's domestic programs. Characteristic of the man who would be president, Haig argued that the potential strategic gain of securing Central America far outweighed the risks of involving the Soviet Union; isolated on this and other issues, the general in the State Department found himself more and more outside the administration's thinking, as the White House opted for modest aid to El Salvador and covert action in the region.

Reagan, moving along the line of least resistance, nonetheless portrayed Soviet proxies on the march in Central America—where only U.S. resolve could hold the apocalyptic line against a row of those proverbial falling dominoes. Or, as the president put it, "If we cannot defend ourselves there, we cannot expect to prevail elsewhere. Our credibility would collapse, our alliances would crumble and the safety of our homeland would be put in jeopardy."

The trouble with El Salvador was that the widespread terrorism practiced by extremists of both the left and the right appeared indistinguishable to the majority of Americans, haunted by the Vietnam experience, who feared greater involvement in the region where fifty thousand people have been killed in the conflict. And despite assurances from diplomats such as Deane Hinton, then U.S. ambassador to El Salvador—"This ain't Vietnam, and it sure as hell better not end the way Vietnam ended"—most Americans shied away from a larger commitment than the fifty-five advisers the president had sent there.

Midway through its first term, the administration appeared amenable to pragmatism, while responding to the region's economic crises (really, sheer underdevelopment) with the Caribbean Basin Initiative (CBI), a modest program consisting of integrated, mutually reinforcing measures in the fields of trade, investment, and financial assistance. (The CBI, defeated by the 97th Congress, was finally passed by the 98th Congress.) On the military front, the White House adopted a lower profile in El Salvador, at the same time covertly arming former followers of Somoza *(Somocistas)* resident in Honduras; from there the *Somocistas*, or contras, raided across the border into Nicaragua from bases in Honduras and Costa Rica to put heat on the *Sandinista* regime and attempt to end its support of the Salvadorean rebels. The net result of Washington's activity in the area ironically increased local support for the *Sandinistas*, inflamed the Nicaraguan-Honduran war, and produced growing hostility in Congress to administration-sponsored aid programs in the region.

In the course of asking for $600 million for maintaining or stepping up support for countries such as El Salvador, the president warned a special joint session of Congress in April 1983 that time was fast running out. Enunciating the so-called Reagan Doctrine for Central America, the president pledged to support "democracy, reform, and human freedom" by using assistance, persuasion, and legitimate leverage to advance "humane democratic systems" in which elections were "open to all, fair and safe." "What I am asking for," the chief executive emphasized in a manner consciously reminiscent of President Truman's plea to Congress in 1947 for aid to Greece and Turkey, "is prompt Congressional approval for the full reprogramming of funds for key economic and security programs so that the people of Central America can hold the line against externally supported aggression." Some thought the president's remarks were a turning point; others were less certain.

No doubt discouraged by the many difficulties inherent in winning congressional approval for his various economic and diplomatic efforts in Central America and perhaps with the 1984 presidential election in mind, the president moved, increasingly or at last visibly, in the direction of a military solution to what he called "the first real communist aggression on the American mainland." He sent the marines. In a show of military force designed to force the left-wing *Sandinistas* of Managua to leave their neighbors alone, the commander in chief dispatched three U.S. navy battle groups to the region, flanking both coasts of Central America; for good measure, as many as four thousand American combat troops were sent to join Honduran forces for the first time in extensive, months-long maneuvers—a "military shield" extending protection to Central American countries friendly to Washington. Reagan also planned to send army engineers and air force transport to Honduras. The plan soon backfired.

Congressional opponents of the White House attacked both the scale and nature of the military exercise. President Miguel de la Madrid of Mexico, a member of the so-called Contadora Group of Latin American leaders who combined together in early 1983 to find a political framework for a negotiated peace in Central America, appealed to Reagan.

Simultaneous with his decision to show the flag, Reagan established an executive commission to advise him on Central American policy. The commission was first proposed in the spring of 1983 by members of Congress from both parties. The National Bipartisan Commission on Central America emerged in July under the leadership of the controversial former secretary of state, Henry Kissinger, who was charged with the tasks of fashioning long-term policy and building short-term support. Clearly, the president had to do something to quiet the growing chorus of critics, particularly House Democrats who in June had threatened to end covert collaboration with the *contras* in Nicaragua, the best-known dirty little secret in Washington. In January 1984, Reagan received the commission's report, which recommended more of everything, more economic aid, more military aid, and greater determination to confront the fact of a Marxist regime in Managua and the threat of one in El Salvador. Moreover, the commission went on, "the use of Nicaragua as a base for Soviet and Cuban efforts to penetrate the rest of the Central American isthmus, with El Salvador the target of first opportunity, gives the conflict there a strategic dimension." For, "the direct involvement of aggressive external forces makes it a challenge to the system of hemispheric security, and quite specifically, to the security interests of the United States. This is the challenge to which the United States must respond." Accordingly, the commissioners concluded,"there might be an argument for doing nothing to help the government of El Salvador. There might be an argument for doing a great deal more. There is, however, no logical argument for giving some aid but not enough."

As the 1984 presidential election campaign approached, the administration stepped up its covert war against Nicaragua. The reaction was at once swift and ironic as news of the CIA mining of Nicaraguan ports triggered a heightened public awareness of the degree of direct U.S. involvement in the secret war against Managua. The influential vice-chairman of the Senate Intelligence Committee, Senator Daniel Moynihan (Democrat, New York), resigned in protest at the failure of the CIA to inform Congress of its involvement of Nicaraguan ports. The powerful chairman of the Intelligence Committee, Arizona conservative Senator Barry Goldwater, having already played the fool on the floor of the Senate when he had authoritatively denied the president had approved any mine laying, protested to CIA director William Casey with simple clarity: "I am pissed off."

In the aftermath, the GOP-controlled Senate passed a nonbinding resolution urging that no more U.S. funds be spent to mine Nicaraguan ports—in reality, an act of war. The House of Representatives followed suit, and then Congress adjourned for Easter without voting a dime for the *contras*. By July, the issue of additional aid for the *contras*—the fifteen thousand CIA-backed Nicaraguan antileftist rebels—was all but "dead." In the process, Congress had begun the inevitable task of weighing "the lessons of Vietnam" against the prospect of the consequences of "Who lost El Salvador?"

Meanwhile, President Reagan set out to eliminate a perceived Soviet threat from another part of the Caribbean. On October 25, 1983, two days after the terrorist attack on marine headquarters in Beirut, the president ordered the invasion of the Caribbean Island of Grenada, the once sleepy tourist haven, barely eighty miles off Venezuela, in order to forestall the installation of a militant pro-Marxist regime with close ties to Havana and Moscow. Triggered by the disintegration of the government of Grenada, following the murder of the prime minister and members of his cabinet, as well as concern to ensure the safety of one thousand Americans (most of them medical students trapped on the island), the invasion marked the first time since the end of the Vietnam War that the United States had committed its troops to a combat attack. By December all American combat troops had withdrawn, their mission accomplished. "We got there just in time," explained the president to a sympathetic nation, "Grenada, we were told, was a friendly island paradise for tourists. It wasn't. It was a Soviet-Cuban colony, being readied as a major military bastion to export terror and undermine democracy." American casualties totaled eighteen killed in action and one hundred sixteen wounded.

"You Ain't Seen Nothin' Yet"

The 1984 presidential election was played out against the background of a resurgent American economy for which the president and the GOP readily took credit. After the worst recession since the 1930s, the country's GNP rose by nearly 5 percent in 1983 and at an annual rate of 8.6 percent in the first half of 1984. Some 6.5 million jobs had been created between the end of 1982 and November 1984. At 7.4 percent, the unemployment rate was slightly below that inherited by Reagan when he assumed office in 1981, thus depriving the Democrats of the claim that the jobless rate had not been brought down below the level of the Carter administration. Equally significant, economic expansion under the Reagan White House had proved disinflationary: prices rose at an annual rate of only 3.2 percent in 1983, down from 6.1 percent in 1982 and 13.3 percent in 1980. High interest rates at home and a towering budget deficit failed to detract from the generally favorable image the public had of the administration. However one assessed the figures, the identification of the president with the return to "good times" made the incumbent an odds-on favorite to retain the White House.

The Democratic National Convention, meeting in San Francisco in July, nominated former Vice-President Walter ("Fritz") Mondale on the first ballot, defeating a late bid by Senator Gary Hart of Colorado. The fifty-six-year-old liberal from Minnesota was the son of a Methodist minister whose Norwegian ancestry dated back to the Vikings. Inward and a very private person, the former protégé of Hubert Humphrey had the unenviable task of reuniting the Democratic party in the wake of one of the most turbulent periods in the history of American politics. He was rejected by 61 percent of the voters in the Democratic primaries while turning back the dual challenge of Senator Hart and black leader Jesse Jackson of Chicago. Hart, a forty-four-year-old Denver lawyer, set off a chain reaction that transformed the campaign with an electrifying upset primary victory in New Hampshire, while Jackson, a forty-two-year-old civil rights activist and protest candidate, drew black voters away from Mondale.

In a dramatic gesture a week before the convention, Mondale named Representative Geraldine Ferraro of New York—the first woman candidate of a major political party for vice-presidential or presidential office—as his running mate. A lawyer, mother, and wife of a millionaire property developer, the three-term Queens congresswoman brought a new dimension to the national ticket, prompting predictions that her selection could well make the presidential contest a very close race. Determined in appearance and smooth in delivery, the Italian-American Ferraro nicely complemented the less telegenic Mondale whose own campaign had been based on traditional Democratic party ties and machine politics.

Meanwhile, fully convinced that the president could not lose the November election, the Republicans gathered in Dallas in August and nominated Reagan and Bush unopposed. Reagan, who never once mentioned Mondale by name, observed the choice in November was not just between two parties, but between two visions of the future: "their government of pessimism, fear and limits; ours of hope, confidence and growth." In adopting its most right-wing policy platform in one hundred thirty years, the GOP offered the American people a sharp choice.

The Republican platform, approved by acclaim in Dallas, flatly opposed tax increases to reduce the nation's budget deficit (running at about $175 billion), advocating instead further tax cuts by increasing individual deductions and repealing the windfall profits tax on oil companies. The Democratic platform, written largely by the people who had engineered Mondale's nomination victory, saw tax increases as an integral part of any deficit solution; specifically, it sought a 15 percent minimum corporate tax, rescission of some of Reagan's 1981 tax cuts, less defense spending, and development of a program to cut health care costs. In the area of arms control and foreign policy, the GOP advocated continued production of all current nuclear weapons and major defense systems, including the Star Wars system to shoot down incoming enemy missiles. For their part, the Democrats sought a mutual, verifiable nuclear weapons freeze with the Kremlin and cancellation of the MX missile and B-1 bomber. In Central America, the Republicans wanted to maintain the status quo while the Democrats favored fewer military exercises in the region, aid to El Salvador contingent upon improvement of human rights there, and termination of funds for the guerillas fighting the Nicaraguan government. Closer to home, the GOP continued to abhor the Equal Rights Amendment while expressing disfavor with abortion; on its side, the Democratic party urged passage of the ERA and strengthening programs for minorities and the poor. The lines were clearly drawn.

Reagan rarely looked anything but a winner. A television joke about bombing the Soviet Union during a voice-level test raised a murmur but his steamroller only really slowed after the first presidential debate. In his first encounter with Mondale, which was devoted to domestic matters and screened on nationwide television, the president badly faltered and showed signs of his age (at seventy-three years old, he was the oldest man ever to serve in that office). But by the second debate, devoted to foreign affairs, the more relaxed and rehearsed incumbent had it all together and was well prepared to fend off his challenger. A week before voting day, the polls gave Mondale the lead in only six out of fifty states; on the day itself, the roof fell in on the Minnesotan.

In the largest victory in American political history, the president defeated his opponent by a popular vote of 53,354,037 (59 percent) to 36,884,260 (41 percent) and an electoral count of 525 to 13, sweeping everything except the District of Columbia and Minnesota. Only one president before Reagan—Richard Nixon in 1972—ever carried forty-nine states; only Lyndon Johnson in 1964 won more of the popular vote. Reagan swept not only every region of the country but every age group and nearly every demographic voting bloc, including a sizable share of union households, Catholics, and southern whites, though he lost out among blacks and Jews. Even Geraldine Ferraro appeared to have hurt Mondale at the polls, with 54 percent of female voters pulling the lever for Reagan, no doubt unimpressed with the congresswoman's explanation of her family's financial affairs borne out by the postelection indictment of her husband. For all this, however, the president was unable to translate his historic victory into significantly increasing his party's margin in the Senate where the Republicans suffered a net loss of two seats (53–47). The Democrats easily kept control of the House of Representatives (266–167), which they had now held for most of the past fifty years.

Still, none could discount the overwhelming public endorsement of Reagan's genial, patriotic leadership and his policies of peace-through-strength abroad and free enterprise at home. Acknowledging victory, the president observed: "America's best days lie ahead. You ain't seen nothin' yet." Presumably he had in mind the completion in his second term of "the conservative revolution" he started in the first, hoping to establish the Republicans as the majority party for the rest of the century. This change would create a different America, though not necessarily a better one.

Suggested Readings

Bartlett, Bruce R. *Reaganomics: Supply Side Economics in Action*. 1981.

Cannon, Lon. *Reagan*. 1982.

Diederich, Bernard. *Somoza—And the Legacy of U.S. Involvement in Central America*. 1983.

Drew, Elizabeth. *Portrait of an Election: The 1980 Presidential Campaign*. 1983.

Evans, Rowland and Novak, Robert. *The Reagan Revolution*. 1981.

Ferguson, Thomas and Rogers, Joel, eds. *The Hidden Election: Politics and Economics in the 1980 Presidential Campaign*. 1981.

Greenshaw, Wayne. *Elephants in the Cottonfields: Ronald Reagan and the New Republican South*. 1982.

Greider, William. *Sentimental Education: The Education of David Stockman and Other Americans*. 1982.

Haig, Jr., Alexander M. *Caveat: Realism, Reagan and Foreign Policy*. 1984.

Kirkpatrick, Jeane J. *Dictatorships and Double Standards*. 1982.

Lekachman, Robert. *Greed Is Not Enough: Reaganomics*. 1982.

Melanson, Richard A. , ed. *Neither Cold War Nor Detente: Soviet American Relations in the 1980s*. 1982.

Quester, George H. *American Foreign Policy: The Lost Consensus*. 1982.

Reagan, Ronald (with Richard G. Hubler). *Where's the Rest of Me?* 1965.

Reinhard, David W. *The Republican Right Since 1945*. 1983.

Roberts, Paul C. *The Supply-Side Revolution: An Insider's Account of Policymaking in Washington*. 1984.

Scheer, Robert. *With Enough Shovels: Reagan, Bush and Nuclear War*. 1982.

Smith, Hedrick et al. *Reagan: The Man, the President*. 1981.

Talbott, Strobe. *Deadly Gambits: The Reagan Administration and the Stalemate in Nuclear Arms Control*. 1984.

Tsongas, Paul. *The Road from Here*. 1981.

Tucker, Robert W. *The Purposes of American Power*. 1981.

Appendix

U. S. Population

Census Year	
1940	131,669,275
1950	150,687,361
1960	178,464,236
1970	204,765,770
1980	226,500,000

Presidential Elections

Election	Candidates	Parties	Popular Vote	Electoral Vote
1944	FRANKLIN D. ROOSEVELT	Democratic	25,602,504 (52.8%)	432
	Thomas E. Dewey	Republican	22,006,285 (44.5%)	919
1948	HARRY S. TRUMAN	Democratic	24,105,812 (49.5%)	303
	Thomas E. Dewey	Republican	21,970,065 (34.1%)	189
	J. Strom Thurmond	States' Rights		
		Democrative	1,169,063 (2.4%)	
	Henry A. Wallace	Progressive	1,157,172 (2.4%)	39
1952	DWIGHT D. EISENHOWER	Republican	33,936,234 (55.2%)	442
	Adlai E. Stevenson	Democratic	27,314,992 (44.5%)	89
1956	DWIGHT D. EISENHOWER	Republican	35,590,472 (57.4%)	457
	Adlai E. Stevenson	Democratic	26,022,752 (42%)	73
1960	JOHN F. KENNEDY	Democratic	34,226,731 (49.9%)	303
	Richard Nixon	Republican	27,178,188 (49.6%)	219
1964	LYNDON B. JOHNSON	Democratic	43,129,484 (61.1%)	486
	Barry M. Goldwater	Republican	27,178,188 (38.5%)	52
1968	RICHARD M. NIXON	Republican	31,785,480 (43.4%)	301
	Hubert H. Humphrey, Jr.	Democratic	31,275,166 (42.7%)	191
	George C. Wallace	American		
		Independent	9,906,473 (13.5%)	46
1972	RICHARD M. NIXON	Republican	47,169,911 (60.6%)	520
	George S. McGovern	Democratic	29,170,383 (37.5%)	17
1976	JIMMY CARTER	Democratic	40,276,040 (50.1%)	297
	Gerald Ford	Republican	38,532,630 (48%)	241
1980	RONALD W. REAGAN	Republican	42,951,045 (51%)	489
	Jimmy Carter	Democratic	34,600,037 (41%)	49
1984	RONALD W. REAGAN	Republican	53,354,037 (59%)	525
	Walter Mondale	Democratic	36,884,260 (41%)	13

Index

The Changing of America: 1945 to the Present was copyedited by Susan Nagel. Production editor was B. W. Barrett. The cover was designed by Roger Eggers. The text was proofread by Elizabeth Rubenstein and Carolee Lipsey. The index was compiled by Sue Baugh. The book was typeset by Prairie Graphics and printed and bound by McNaughton & Gunn, Inc.